RAISING AN HIGHLY SENSITIVE CHILD

Understanding Symptoms, Improve Your Parenting Strategies And Help Your Kid Handle This Gift, Even At School And With Friends.

Boys And Girls' Discipline Guidelines

The following manuscript has been produced to help its readers in making some of the best decisions related to the subject. The data offered herein is not only accurate but also supportive of the topics that have been discussed. Therefore, regardless of that, when purchasing this manuscript, the individual is considered to be an adult who has consented to own the book. Also, it is important to note that the author of the chapters of this book is not liable for any harm that may befall someone after they have read and understood the contents of this book. Apart from that, it's also important to note that the chapters of this manuscript carry a lot of useful content that will be helpful in assisting its readers to be knowledgeable. Therefore, while gaining information, it becomes vital for people to read more about the usefulness of the data and not focus on how harmful it may be. Other than that, the book has been produced with the intention of offering significant information for the people who shall be reading.

Table of Contents

Introduction

The highly sensitive child is one of the 15-20% of children born with a nervous system that is highly aware and quick to react to everything. Such children are incredibly responsive to the environment, whether it is the lighting, sounds, smells or overload mood of the people in their situations.

These kids are often gifted intellectually, creatively and emotionally demonstrating genuine compassion at early ages. The downside is that these intensely perceptive kids also get overwhelmed easily by crowds, noises, new situations, sudden changes and the emotional distress of others. These kids need extra care and feeding so they can learn how to see their sensitivity as a strength and being empowering themselves with tools to tap into their sensitivity, such as insight, creativity and empathy, while simultaneously learning how to manage their rich emotional lives.

In most cases High Sensitivity is inherited. However, it is also true that sensitivity can be impacted through certain life experiences. Traumas at an early age may push a child with mild sensitivity to demonstrate traits of High Sensitivity, while exposure to certain stimuli over a long time can decrease someone's sensitivity to that stimuli.

What is highly sensitivity NOT

High sensitivity is NOT a psychological disorder. It is not being shy or neurotic, nor does it necessarily indicate introversion. To clarify the differences, let's look at these conditions more closely:

- Shyness is a feeling of timidity, apprehension, or discomfort in at least some social situations. Shyness is a learned behavior. Because HSPs prefer to look before entering new situations, they are often incorrectly labeled as "shy." It is natural for an HSP to "hang back" and observe new situations. It is not aversion; it is simply time to deeply process new sensory data.
- Neurosis is a functional behavior disorder with no apparent underlying cause for the feelings of ill-health it engenders. Neuroses include a number of affective disorders, such as anxiety, depression, and obsessive states. When an HSP approaches stimuli overload (more on this state later), their shutdown behaviors, which may include anxiety, depression, or anger, may appear to others to have no apparent underlying cause and thus be a neurosis. Rather, the state has a very real and physiological cause to the HSP.
- Introverts are deeply concerned with the inner world of the mind. They enjoy thinking, exploring their thoughts and feelings. Being around people drains the energy of an introvert, while time spent alone re-energizes them. About 25-40% of the general population is introverted, while about 70% of HSPs are introverts. So while there is a high correlation between being Highly Sensitive and being introverted, they are not the same thing.

Highly sensitivity is a normal, natural and healthy condition of nervous system. There is nothing wrong being highly sensitive. There is only something uncommon about being highly sensitive.

PART I
Understanding and Recognising Symptoms

Chapter 1 - The Most Common Traits of a HSC

Is your child always on the brink of tears? Does your child suddenly go all quiet, or shy away from people and situations? Do you feel your child's reactions are a little too emotional? If your answers are yes, then your child could be sensitive. A sensitive child needs to be dealt with delicately.

If you feel your parenting skills are resulting in extreme reactions from your child, maybe it's time to do a reality check. Read on to know if your child is highly sensitive and what you need to do to handle him with care.

Signs Of A Highly Sensitive Child

A highly sensitive child, as the name suggests, is more susceptible to the people and situations around him. Here are a few highly sensitive child traits you may notice in your child.

1. Reacts Emotionally

Your highly sensitive child will react with emotionally to almost everything. A simple visit to a pet store could leave him feeling miserable for the animals there. A stern look from you could reduce him to tears. Being highly sensitive also makes your child empathize with others. He may feel so bad about others' problems that he wants to go out of his way to help them. He may worry too much about others and want to make things right for them.

2. Broods Over Failures

If your child is highly sensitive, he will delve deeper into things than most other children of his age do. For your child, a simple event like failure to achieve a particular target will not be just that. He broods over the matter, thinking why he did not realize the mistake in time, and what he could have done about it. This could result in stress and anxiety.

3. Takes Things Personally

For your child, being highly emotional means that everything that happens is personal. Your child will react to everything in a way where he feels whatever others say is applicable to him only.

4. Difficulty In Making A Choice

A common trait among highly sensitive children is the difficulty in taking a decision. Your child will look into various details and subtleties, making it difficult for him to select. For instance, if asked to choose a flavor of ice cream, your child will take a long time to decide. In certain cases, he may find it difficult to choose, like something as simple as choosing a partner in a game.

5. Feels Guilty

If your child feels that he has taken a wrong decision he will feel extremely guilty. He will ponder over too much into the reasons.

No matter what you say or do, he would not come out of it for a long time.

6. Displays A Tough Exterior

You don't want to be on the wrong side for your sensitive kids. They may be mad at you for a month. They may be hurt by something you did or said and will simply hold on it than expressing it to you.

7. Well-mannered And Polite

Kids who are sensitive are well behaved and also expect to be in similar surroundings.

8. They Read People Well

Sensitive kids have a keen sense of observation and know people well. They observe character traits and gather an accurate story of who the person is.

9. They Love Animals

Kids who are sensitive develop a special bond with animals wherein they trust them completely. It's not just trust they are also sensitive to the needs of animals and take extra care of it.

10. They Ask A Lot Of Questions

Kids generally asк a lot of questions. At times the questions can be irritating and may be personal. But in general the questions may leave you with a sense of positive thought.

11. They Are Calculative And Taкe Firm Decisions

Sensitive кids generally maкe decisions after putting in a lot of going through a lot of emotions. They do things for a reason and if they fail, they are often left in self-doubt. Once they have taкen a decision, they usually stand by it even if they are alone and can be disheartened at times to see how insensitive others can be.

12. They Feel Accountable And Admit Their Mistaкes

Sensitive кids not only try and study their environment but also continually evaluate themselves and кeep their emotions in checк. If they feel they have done a mistaкe they don't hesitate to admit it and they always appreciate others for small acts.

13. They taкe in more sensory information from their environment than other кids

Highly sensitive children hear faint sounds, detect subtle smells and notice details in drawings and architecture that other кids ignore. They may find certain foods too flavourful, or can't stand to wear certain fabrics.

14. They process information more thoroughly.

Their creativity and intuition spring from this rich, deeply-reflective inner life.

15. They have a keen empathy for others.

Highly sensitive kids take on the emotions of those around them, sharing in their highs and lows.

16. They are easily overstimulated.

Compared to other children, sensitive kids tire more rapidly and need more rest or down time.

17. They are prone to sudden tantrums and meltdowns, often precipitated by information overload or emotional overload.

Situations meant to be a treat for a child – an indoor playground, a birthday party or a day at a theme park – can quickly become an ordeal for sensitive kids.

Taken together, highly sensitive kids perceive more, ponder more and feel more. And they more quickly reach their limits.

Habits Of A Highly Sensitive Child

- Highly sensitive kids with their heart, as they sympathize others. Logic doesn't apply.

- They are talkative and would like to be appreciated by their peers. But when people offer
- advice they may be easily offended.
- These children prefer to be alone, and spend more time by themselves.
- They work hard to ensure that they are perfect in their work.
- They trust their instinct while taking a decision.
- Sensitive kids have a keen sense of observation and understand people well.
- They love animals.
- They ask a lot of questions.
- These kids do not like horror movies.
- While they prefer to work alone, they can also be good team players.
- They like to work in closed environments where they are not visible to others.

Chapter 2 - Caution, Consequences, and Conscientiousness (not shyness)

Even when calm and happy, highly sensitive children tend to stand out from the group, if only because they don't participate. They watch the action from the sidelines, are reluctant to speaĸ up in class and eschew the pressure of team sports.

All in all these ĸids are far from gung ho about new experiences: they liĸe predictability. And so they worry ahead of time about sleepovers, vacations away from home, the start of a new school year, school field trips and Christmas gatherings, any of which might precipitate headaches, stomach aches, nightmares or difficulty eating or sleeping.

Not surprisingly then, highly sensitive children are often labelled "shy," "anxious" or "slow to adapt to change." But these labels don't fairly reflect what's going on inside.

Highly sensitive children could be better described as having a strong sense of caution and consequences, and being highly conscientiousness.

A strong sense of caution

One of the scientific models for the cause of sensitivity, is that sensitive persons have a very active 'behavioural inhibition system'. I prefer to call this system in the brain the 'pause-to-checĸ system' because that is what it really does. It is designed to looĸ at the situation you are in and see if it is similar to any past situations stored in your memory. Faced with an unfamiliar experience, an HSC wants to check it out, and if forced to proceed, may protest, not enjoy it, or refuse this 'pleasure' altogether. Remember, too, that any new experience means an intimidating flood of unfamiliar sensory experiences. Most HSCs seem to be poor adapters, but in reality they are being asked to adapt to too much. They are overwhelmed, or afraid of being overwhelmed, by all the new stimulation that must be processed before they can relax.

A keen awareness of potential consequences

Because of their mature thinking skills, a highly sensitive child can well imagine the full impact of potential outcomes, and they typically want to mitigate risk. News reports of fires and break-ins will get them fretting about the safety measures in their own home. One of the biggest tasks for a sensitive person, is to live courageously with a full awareness of the unpleasant possibilities in life. HSCs cannot deny these as well as others can.

Conscientiousness that trips them up

Highly sensitive children are conscientious almost to a fault. They want to "do the right thing," and take personal slip ups and mistakes harder than most. Being so "mistake conscious" makes them self-conscious. It's difficult for them to shrug off embarrassment over "putting a foot wrong" in public. They don't think, That just proves I'm human; they think, That just proves I'm inadequate. Public speaking, music recitals, spelling bees, significant assignments and written exams can fill them with

real dread; so much so that they may perform below their real
level of ability.

Chapter 3 - The highly sensitive child and behavioral inhibition

Most children have an easy and outgoing nature. They are curious about new people and places, кeen to explore and try out new and interesting toys, they are adventurous but not fearless, and when upset they can easily be comforted and recover quicкly from disappointments and setbacкs.

Other children are born with a more cautious temperament and respond to new situations and people with wariness, they are slow to warm-up and are easily distressed by unfamiliar, unpredictable and unexpected events. They taкe longer to recover when upset.

The phrases "highly sensitive child" (HSC) and "behavior inhibition" (BI) describing children as very aware and quicк to react to everything.

These differences in children's nature are called temperament traits and are determined by biological differences in the way in which the brain records, processes, interprets and responds to information from the environment which in turn determines an individual's behavior and learning.

Behavioral inhibition: the cautious/fearful child

Behavioral inhibition is a specific temperament trait first identified and described by Jerome Kagan in the 80's. Children with an inhibited temperament are cautious, restrained and even fearful in response to unfamiliar people, objects and situations.

Inhibited children have a very active fear system. The regions of the brain that assess signals from within the body (such as body sensations) and information from the environment for the presence of potential threat or danger, are unusually alert and reactive. Things that are new, unfamiliar, different or difficult are interpreted as being threatening or dangerous. This creates a fear response and activates the body's fear behaviors of fight, flee or freeze.

Cautious/fearful infants may be fussy, react strongly to any changes such as being undressed, are difficult to calm, react strongly to strangers or new situations. They also are very sensitive to being wet, hungry, or in discomfort. These infants become easily over-aroused and distressed when there is a lot going on around them. As they get older they may develop a strong fear of strangers, cling to parents in new situations and develop separation anxiety.

As the cautious/fearful child gets a little older he/she may avoid activities that seem difficult, physically challenging or complex. Intense physical activity such as running or jumping creates strong sensations of effort within the body – and the child may interpret these as being threatening and so avoid physical activity.

The orienting response and the autonomic system
The orienting response is the brain's way of responding to novel and interesting events in the environment.

When a new event occurs the brain maкes a decision as to whether it is safe to approach and investigate, or is not safe and needs to be avoided. This is followed by the orienting response which includes activation of the autonomic system affecting breathing, heart rate and blood supply to the muscles and changes in muscle tone in preparation for action.

Stephen Poges describes three ways the autonomic system can respond the events, each with a different set of body responses:

The social engagement system - mediated by the polyvagal system (a part of the parasympathetic system) orients the organism towards a situation and promotes engagement.

The sympathetic system primes the body for action and provides the impetus for muscle work. In situations of danger, it is the sympathetic system that promotes flight or fight responses - whichever is more appropriate.

The primitive parasympathetic system primes the body for freezing in situations where not responding and being very still has survival value.

The three systems in action

If the child finds the situation interesting and challenging she will orient her attention towards what she encounters, her attention will become focused and the physiological systems needed for action will be mobilized with just enough energy for the task, and in social situations she will act with positive facial expressions and focused attention to the human voice. The child experiences the event in a positive manner and feels good about herself.

However if the child perceives the situation to be threatening, the brain's fear/avoidance systems prime the sympathetic system towards the flight or fight responses. The heart starts to beat faster, breathing rate increases, there is a sensation of butterflies in the stomach. These responses create the feeling of either excitement or of fear.

The other way in which the child may react to a threatening situation is to "freeze" - the body is primed for disengagement, for being very still, not responding and not being noticed. This is the most basic and primitive way for an organism to respond to threat. The child simply refuses to engage with a situation, and no amount of persuasion will get her to change her mind.

Fear creates unpleasant sensations in the body

Fear is experienced both in the mind and in the body: it may be experienced as a feeling of tightness and constriction in the throat, tightness or pressure on the chest wall or butterflies in the stomach.

Most young children can identify where in their bodies they experience their fear. Ask your child "Where do you feel scared?" Point to the throat, chest, and tummy and ask "Here, here or here?" Each child has a particular way of experiencing fear.

All young children show a fear response when confronted by frightening or very unusual situations. They will respond by staying close to their parents, and exhibit facial expressions of fear, crying and a refusal to investigate and approach.

However cautious/fearful children may show fear responses in situations that are not particularly threatening or frightening but are unfamiliar, different, unpredictable or unexpected.

There are also a group of children with higher levels of behavioral inhibition (high BI) who show more extreme fear behaviors that may include signs of distress and crying, clinging, withdrawal from the situation, complete refusal to participate even in situations with low threat level.

Children with high BI show patterns of dysregulated behavior. They show fear responses even in situations that are not threatening and at times their fearful behavior and levels of distress are extreme and continue long after the threat has been removed.

High BI children and those with a dysregulated fear responses (DF) have a fear system that is highly vigilant and constantly on the lookout for threats.

The Sensory Processing Disorder (SPD) Foundation describes sensory processing as follows: "Sensory Processing Disorder (SPD, formerly known as "sensory integration dysfunction") is a condition that exists when sensory signals don't get organized into appropriate responses. Pioneering occupational therapist and neuroscientist A. Jean Ayres, PhD, likened SPD to a neurological "traffic jam" that prevents certain parts of the brain from receiving the information needed to interpret sensory information correctly. A person with SPD finds it difficult to process and act upon information received through the senses, which creates challenges in performing countless everyday tasks."

The SPD Foundation website goes on to make the following claim: Motor clumsiness, behavioral problems, anxiety, depression, school failure, and other impacts may result if the disorder is not treated effectively.

In contrast to the large body of scientific evidence that links a fearful temperament style (BI) to a range of difficult behaviors, including aberrant responses to sensory inputs, there is no evidence to show that "motor clumsiness, behavioral problems, anxiety, depression, school failure" are caused by difficulties with sensory processing or integration.

At any given time an individual's interpretation and responses to sensory information (proprioception, enteroception, touch, visual and auditory signals) depends on the situation, general state of positive or negative emotional tone, expectations, plans for action and many other factors. All these factors together play a role in selecting what information is important (salient) what gets filtered out, what gets attention, and what gets used in pursuit of present goals.

Feeling physically unsafe and in danger of falling

Some cautious/fearful children are particularly sensitive to danger and feeling physically unsafe. In particular they are fearful of trying new activities that have an element of risk. Fearful children may avoid climbing on play equipment, jungle gyms, trees, walking on raised surfaces, climbing up steep slopes, playing on see-saws and roundabouts, ladders and slides. Riding in an elevator or on an escalator may provoke a fear response.

New situations

Highly sensitive children who are cautious/fearful children usually approach new situations or activities very hesitantly, and seem nervous or uncomfortable. They get upset at being left in new situations for the first time and may take many days to adjust to kindergarten, preschool, or childcare.

Busy and noisy environments

Cautious/fearful children often dislike situations that include lots of people moving around, unexpected noises and events. They are particularly sensitive to unexpected events. They do not like surprises. They prefer to be in control. They are also less good at predicting what is going to happen next which means that things that most children expect to happen in the normal course of events turn out to be unexpected for children with high behavioral inhibition and high fear arousal. When walking down the aisle of a busy supermarket with many people walking in in different directions we natural look ahead, notice who is coming directly towards us and take action to avoid a collision. We know how to pay attention to the most important information and filter out unnecessary information and manage to walk along the aisles without bumping into people and things. A child with high fear arousal may not be able to filter all out unimportant noise and visual information or be able to select the most important information; they become overwhelmed and are not able to plan their path ahead, instead the child bumps into people and things and may lose sight of mom who has gone around the corner with the trolley.

Loud, unpredictable and unexpected noise

Some children are very sensitive to noise levels, especially unexpected and unpredictable noises. Thunderstorms may provoke a strong fear response. A child may develop a particular dislike and fear reaction to particular sounds such as sirens and when someone shouts loudly. If a child is a worrier he may react strongly to sounds of loud sirens going off close by: what does it mean, what has gone wrong, is there a fire, are we in danger? Children with high levels of arousal may find too much background noise unpleasant.

Fear of unfamiliar adults

Some children may be particularly withdrawn or fearful in the presence of strangers. The child may be very shy and refuse to engage with friendly unfamiliar adults even in a safe environment.

Shyness with other children

Cautious/fearful children may be shy when first meeting new children and reluctant to approach a group of unfamiliar children to ask to join in. They may prefer to watch other children, rather than join in their games.

Hypersensitivity to tactile inputs

Some children develop a dislike to the feel of clothing with certain textures or clothing that is tight and fits closely. They may also develop a dislike to the feeling of different surfaces and textures under their feet or to the feel of soft and sticky stuff on their hands. The reason for the development of tactile hypersensitivity is not clear. The argument that it is due to a sensory processing disorder does not take into account the complex nature of how the brain filters, selects and weights sensory information.

The highly sensitive child, behavioral inhibition and anxiety

Behavioral inhibition as a temperament style is related to a child's fear responses to unfamiliar and unpredictable situations as well as familiar events that are perceived as threatening.

Some children with high BI are at risk for later development of anxiety disorders including generalized anxiety disorder and social anxiety disorder.

What are the signs of anxiety in children?

- finding it hard to concentrate
- not sleeping, or waking in the night with bad dreams
- not eating properly
- quickly getting angry or irritable, and being out of control during outbursts
- constantly worrying or having negative thoughts about things such as
- feeling tense and fidgety, or using the toilet often
- always crying
- being clingy all the time (when other children are ok)
- complaining of tummy aches and feeling unwell
- may be very hard on themselves and strive for perfection.
- may seek constant approval or reassurance from others.

If you think your child may have an anxiety disorder it is important to talk to your child's primary care physician/GP.

Varied experience promotes coping behaviors

It is helpful to remember that fearful children are particularly sensitive to events that are new, unfamiliar and unpredictable.

Children who have been encouraged to explore, take risks and take on challenges develop better coping skills and learn to moderate their tendency to withdraw or avoid situations they perceive to be threatening. A broad range of experience also means that the young child is faced with fewer unfamiliar situations and is better at predicting what will happen next.

A young child who has been encouraged to climb up onto the sofa as a toddler, has learned to climb up onto kitchen chair to reach a shelf, has been helped up to climb up the ladder of a high slide and been encouraged to slide down, and has played rough and tumble games with daddy is used to dealing with what can appear to be physically dangerous situations and also enjoys to mixture of fear and excitement that goes with tackling new physical challenges. The same child may be cautious but does not experience excessive fear responses when he/she goes to a new outdoor play area that has many new and interesting climbing apparatuses.

Children who have been given lots of opportunities to get their hands dirty and sticky from an early age are happy to play messy games as pre-schoolers. Messy play starts when infants are allowed to play with their food: smearing yogurt or porridge on the table, eating soft food with their fingers, and feeding themselves with a spoon even when the food mostly does not reach the mouth.

Sensitivity to unexpected and unpredictable events

High BI children often have heightened levels of fear arousal, which makes them extremely sensitive to any events in the environment that are unexpected. They do not like situations that are unpredictable. A child in a state of heightened fearful arousal is usually busy monitoring what is happening in the here-and-now and this also interferes with his/her ability to predict what will happen next. This means that the environment becomes even more uncertain.

A typically developing child sitting at the top of a high slide anticipates the sensations that go with the upcoming fast descent down the slide. A fearful child may be paying attention to the anxiety that goes with being so high off the ground that he does not anticipate the fast movement of his buttocks on the slide or the rush of air past his face as his body makes its rapid descent. These sensations are unexpected even though he has been down the slide several times before.

Fearful children tend to form strong negative associations

When two events happen more or less at the same time we tend to form a strong association between the two: a drink of cold water on a hot day relieves your thirst and tastes good, A negative association happens when an unpleasant or threatening event occurs at the same time as a neutral or low threat event. *"I am happily eating a plate of oats porridge when there is a very loud, fear provoking noise out on the street. I get a very big fight, my heart starts to pound and there is a feeling of tightness in my chest which lasts for quite a long time"*. A connection is made in my brain between eating oats porridge and all the unpleasant sensations that were caused by the loud bang. As a result have developed a really strong dislike of oats porridge.

Tendency to exaggerated fear learning

Fearful children can develop a strong dislike and fear response after just one unpleasant or threatening experience.

- *A single unpleasant experience with a big dog may provoke a fear of all dogs.*
- *A fall of the lowest rung of the jungle gym may lead to refusal to climb on the jungle gym again.*

Negative responses to strong sensations from their bodies

The brain continuously monitors information from the body. This information comes from the many sensors in the skin, fascial structures, joints and muscles, blood vessels, internal organs, and vestibular system. Depending on the context the sensitivity of the sensors in all these structures can be adjusted to provide more or less information.

Much of the time we are not aware of the incoming information from our bodies. We sit on a chair without being aware of the pressure of the buttocks on the seat, we walk without taking any notice information from the soles of our feet as they make contact with the ground, and the regular beating of our hearts and movement of the chest wall as we breathe goes unnoticed.

However, any changes in the intensity of the information coming from our bodies usually reaches our attention and may provoke an emotional response.

"As adults we often know what is causing the increase in sensations: we expect the muscles to ache a little, the heart to

beat faster and our breathing to become labored when we engage in effortful physical activity”.

Cautious/fearful children are often highly sensitive to such increased sensory input from the body sensors and may respond with increased fear arousal.

“A little bit of discomfort from muscles that are working hard or being stretched, a slight increase in the rate of the heartbeat, a bit of distension in the abdomen after a large meal may feel threatening and provoke a disproportional emotional response”.
Children may avoid any effortful physical activity because they want to avoid these sensations of effort that are perceived as threatening. .

A tendency focus attention on threatening events

Some cautious/fearful children have a tendency to hone in on any sensations arising from their bodies or sensory information from the environment which they perceive as a threat. This is termed attentional bias to threat.

The perceived threat grabs their attention and they have difficulty shifting the focus of their attention away from the threat. Maintaining attention focus on a perceived threat increases arousal levels which in turn increases the tendency to focus on the threat.

Perceived threats that may be lead to strong attentional bias include sensory inputs from the environment such as unexpected and unpredictable loud noises, unfamiliar people, unfamiliar animals, fear provoking objects such as a toy spider or noisy unpredictable toy.

"I sometimes play a jumping game where a child jumps over a gap from one cushion to another. The gap is a pretend river and in the river there is a toy wooden crocodile. If the child falls into the river he gets eaten by the crocodile. Every now and then I meet a child who refuses to jump until I take away the wooden crocodile.Usually I just put it back on the shelf and the child forgets about it, but one little boy became so focused on the wooden crocodile that I had to put it out of sight in a cupboard and lock the door before he would continue with the game".

Sensitivity to mistakes and failure

From a very young age children monitor the success or failure of their attempts to achieve a goal. Success tends to tweak the brain's reward systems which provides the child with that good feeling that goes with success. The more challenging the task, the greater the sense of achievement.

Young children are also very aware of failed attempts and in most instances use this information to adapt their actions on the next trial and in this way learn from their mistakes.

Cautious/inhibited on the other hand often experience failure as threatening

Instead of learning from failed attempts they get upset, give up and may refuse to try again. They may also become very upset when they make a mistake.

This is a real problem because without repeated practice and a good mixture of both successful and failed attempts learning does not happen.

Fear of failure leads to freezing and avoidance

Cautious/inhibited children often respond to their fear of failure by finding ways to avoid doing a task. One avoidance strategy is to simply refuse to engage with the task, and no amount of cajoling and pleading can get them to change their minds. Sometimes children will make a very half-hearted attempt to perform the task and then engage in distracting chatter and sometimes acting silly. Cautious children often become the class clown.

Movement skills and the cautious/fearful child

Learning to perform a new movement based task requires engagement and sustained mental effort to support the emotional and cognitive work needed to approach a new and unfamiliar situation, control and sustain attention, explore ways of achieving the goal and keep going until the goal is achieved, often in the face of frustration and failure. When tackling an unfamiliar task, a child needs to regulate his emotional responses, direct his attention appropriately (effortful control) and call into play a range of thinking skills (executive functions) needed for planning and organizing his actions.

Self-regulation refers to the child's capacity to control the inherent tendency to react to situations in a particular way, such as approach or avoidance, holding back or rushing in. It refers to a child's ability to adapt and control his or her innate responses to stimuli from within the body and from the environment, and the ability to direct and use attention in an appropriate way.

The cautious/fearful child learning a new skill

Cautious/fearful children may find engaging with an unfamiliar task overwhelming. The immediate response, before even considering the task, may be a fear reaction with over-arousal and feelings of anxiety. The child's emotional system may go into panic mode lead to an emotional outburst, but more often the physiological response is to freeze and simply refuse to even try.

Another child may be willing approach the task, but become discouraged at the first hurdle, and not be able to work out what to do next. Or he may narrowly focus his attention on one aspect of the task - get stuck on that and refuse to proceed.

Jess (5 years) likes playing with her collection of 20 piece puzzles. Sometimes she tips all the pieces out on the table and then with great concentration and persistence sorts outs the pieces and builds them all. Recently her mom bought her a new 50 piece puzzle depicting an underwater scene. Together they sat down, tipped out all the pieces and looked at the picture on the box. They started to look for the pieces that made up the large brightly colored fishes but after a few minutes and much to her mom's surprise Jess' initial enthusiasm quickly gave way to an emotional outburst. She wiped the puzzle pieces off the table, called the puzzle stupid and stomped off to her bedroom.

Learning a task that involves physical effort

Cautious/fearful children sometimes over-focuses on the physical sensations from within the body and may react strongly to the feelings of effort that accompany activities that require muscular effort or get the heart beating fast.

Many of the physical activities young children engage in require quite strenuous muscular and cardiovascular exertion.

- Running will also get the heart beating rapidly - and the child finds this unpleasant because he associates this sensation with fear and anxiety.
- Jumping high or far elicits a powerful contraction in the quadriceps muscles, and a feeling of pressure in the knees - and the child finds this unpleasant and dangerous.
- Hanging from the monkey bars is scary because you are a long way from the ground, but it also quite hard on the hands and creates strong activity in the shoulder muscles. It is no wonder that highly sensitive children avoid the monkey bars and climbing frame.

"Molly (aged 6) is a cautious little girl with joint hypermobility. As part of her strength training program I wanted her to do some big jumps from one cushion to another over a gap. This activity requires forceful contraction of the leg muscles to initiate the jump and then to absorb the momentum on landing. Molly did 3 jumps and then moved away and sat on a bench near the door. She refused to try again.

I sat down next to her and talked about how the knees feel when one does a big jump; the muscles have to work very hard and sometimes that feels a little uncomfortable. Molly listened to my explanation but still refused to try again, and in response to my continued efforts to coax her into action she blurted out that her bones felt like they were breaking and she did not want to go to hospital. She also told me that her granny had a fall recently and needed an operation to fix her hip".

By the age of five a young a child with movement difficulties watches his peers doing a range of balance, climbing, agility and ball skills. He expects to be able to do them as well as his friends and gets disheartened when he cannot compete and keep up. What he does not understand is that his peers have invested a great deal of time and effort over a number of years into learning and perfecting these skills. And as a result they are also more agile, stronger and fitter.

Helping very cautious children to overcome their fears

In my work with fearful children who have movement difficulties I am always amazed at how quickly and easily a child can be shifted from fearfulness to courage in the face of physical challenges. As one 6-year-old put it "I have leant to face my fears".

The same child had also learned to enjoy working his muscles hard and to interpret sensations of tiredness in his muscles as a good thing - because "it means that my muscles are working hard enough to make them stronger".

He had learned to put in the extra effort needed to complete a task when his muscles were starting to tire, and the pleasure of pushing himself hard to reach a goal or meet a challenge.

"Michael was nearly five when he first came to see me. He tolerated the assessment tasks for about 20 minutes - then started to whine and wanted to leave. So we switched to games. We played being chased by a lion and did shuttle runs across the room, with me shouting loud warnings about the

lion catching me and encouragement to run faster. When we stopped I encouraged him to feel his heart beating. Yes, it was beating very, very fast because that is what hearts do when one runs. He wanted his mom to feel his heart, and then wanted to feel my heart beating fast. After a little rest he wanted to run again - so that he could feel his heart again.

His perception of his heart beating fast had shifted from being a signal of an anxiety-provoking situation to the sensation of effort, exercise and excitement".

We also did some jumping from one big cushion to another - big jumps across a river. He did a few, then refused to do any more. So we had a conversation about what his knees felt like when he jumped. And my response was "That is what knees feel like when you jump". His mom reported that in the car on the way home Michael was very excited about feeling his knees. "Mom" he said "I can feel my knees". He also did a lot of jumping at home in the week that followed.

Chapter 4 - Noise, Lights, Tags: Hypersensivity and Sensory Processing Disorder

"My 11-year-old daughter has been wearing clothes that seem inappropriate for the weather. It was really hot this past summer, but she wore flannel pajamas at night. When we turned on the fan in her room, she was bothered by the sound. I also found that she doesn't want to turn on the lights in the morning. Does she have sensory issues?"

Whether your daughter has sensory processing disorder (SPD), your attention to her tactile, auditory, and visual challenges will make her more comfortable physically. She'll also be grateful that you take her complaints seriously and try to address them. Here's what I advise.

Pajamas for Sensitive Kids

She may be wearing flannel PJs not for warmth but because they protect her skin from irritating tactile sensations coming from sheets or the fan. Buy some lightweight, all-cotton, soft, smooth (no tags or seams) summer pajamas, such as Hanes long-sleeved cool Dri t-shirts. You might also check out the website Fun and Function for clothes especially made for children with tactile sensitivities. Finally, splurge on the highest-quality cotton sheets (without polyester).

Kids Sensitive to Noise

A white-noise machine may mask the sound of the fan. Some people with auditory challenges recommend sleeping with soft music to block out house sounds.

Kids Sensitive to Light

Many people, with and without SPD, adjust slowly to environmental transitions, such as going from darkness to bright light. It could be that "cool" light bulbs in her bedroom irritate her visual system, so change to incandescent or "warm white" bulbs that disperse a kinder light. If she can get dressed without the lights on, indulge her preference to get dressed in a dimly lit room while her eyes wake up.

Living with hypersensitivity is challenging, especially for children. It affects their fundamental experience of the world around them and – understandably – it's something that many parents and guardians will try to remedy. The problem is – if you don't understand the root cause of the hypersensitivity, most treatments will fail.

Could sensory processing disorder be behind your child's hypersensitivity? Read on as we take a closer look at this complex disorder, the symptoms and treatments.

What exactly is hypersensitivity?

Hypersensitivity can be difficult to get your head around, even
for parents and guardians of children with the disorder. It refers
to having heightened sensitivity to stimulation of the senses.
This can apply to any of the five senses – touch, sight, hearing,
smell and taste – and may even affect multiple senses for some
sufferers. Senses provide humans with a way to view, perceive
and understand life and the world around us. What we see,
taste, feel, taste and smell, moulds our physical understanding
of life – essentially forming our conscious experience. Imagine,
if these sensations were heightened to the extreme, just how
difficult everyday life would suddenly be.

Children with hypersensitivity will often complain about sensory
stimuli that others perceive as ordinary. Whether it's a sound, a
feeling or a smell, it can be almost impossible for them to
control their response to these extreme sensory stimulations.
Even a well-meaning hug can cause a child with hypersensitivity
to lose their temper, which can understandably be difficult for
parents and guardians alike.

Symptoms of hypersensitivity

Children may also suffer from hyposensitivity, which is generally
grouped with hypersensitivity because of how it affects sufferers.
While "hyper" refers to too much sensitivity, "hypo" means there
is too little sensation for any of the five senses. Both disorders
stem from issues in the brain and nervous system. The difficulty
with sensations can make everyday activities overwhelming and
unbearable. It causes children to over or under respond to food,
noise, light, sounds or textures. Because it impacts their basic

experience of the world, it can manifest in almost every facet of a child's life, such as:

- Difficulty with gross motor skills, such as walking clumsily
- Difficulty with fine motor skills like handwriting
- Hearing – Meltdown in response to loud bangs, fireworks or even loud chewing noises at the dinner table
- Aggression – Poor ability to focus due to constant noise and distraction
- Touch – Problems dealing with fabric textures, clothes labels and tight clothing or sand and grass on bare feet, for example
- Food – The taste and textures of certain foods, such as mushy banana, can be difficult to deal with
- No sense of boundaries or personal space
- An unusually high tolerance to pain
- Impaired language development, with difficulty reading aloud
- Overwhelming anxiety when learning something new
- Poor posture or strength
- Poor eye tracking, including hand eye coordination
- A discomfort with heights
- Resistance to change or failure to function or perform when following a strict routine
- Behavioural problems with a broad spectrum of severity
- Overreaction to visual or auditory input – children can be easily misdiagnosed and put on medication for ADHD
- Bad reaction to overstimulation from bright lights, in classrooms for instance
- Certain autistic characteristics

With many of these symptoms, it's common for people to think children are just behaving badly when reacting to sounds, tastes, smells, touch or sights. However, they are actually unable to control their physical and emotional reaction to this information.

So, what's actually behind hypersensitivity and hyposensitivity?

The symptoms occur when sensory stimuli aren't interpreted properly by the brain – and the nervous system as a result. Any information received through the affected senses is heightened or dampened, determining how children respond to it.

At the root of the cause is the Reticular Activating System. This is part of the brain stem, which manages all information that is passed up through the spinal cord. Essentially, it acts as the resistor in the body's neural circuitry. If underdeveloped, it leads to poor management of signals, known as Sensory Processing Disorder.

More on Sensory Processing Disorder (or SPD)

SPD can occur in two ways. Either it results in information overload, leading to stress and fatigue, or a lack of information, leading to poor interpretation of social norms or deficient skills. Because it's such a central part of how we develop, SPD is at the root of a number of issues in both children and adults. This also means children with one issue, such as dyslexia, may be contending with another disorder in some capacity, such as hypersensitivity or developmental coordination disorder. In recent years, Autistic Spectrum disorder has grown as a concept. Science is beginning to note that all these difficulties are often interlinked. SPD is in the same category. It's a form of developmental delay and neuromotor immaturity that can have interlinking disorders and symptoms.

Treating SPD and hypersensitivity

With just a few adjustments to a child's day-to-day life, you can help them better manage the symptoms of hypersensitivity and hyposensitivity. One is to simply raise awareness and improve your understanding of the symptoms, as well as anybody regularly in contact with your child.

Children can also adopt a sensory lifestyle. For example, headphones can be used to regulate noise levels and special lighting can help avoid overstimulation. However, it's best to treat the root cause. By releasing incorrectly retained reflexes, it's possible to alleviate over-stimulation or under-stimulation and remove the blocks of incorrect development. Here is how it can be done:

- Stimulation therapy – eye tracking, balance and sensory tasks
- Auditory processing – train the inner ear muscle with neuro-acoustic training
- Sensory integration therapy – comprising visual, auditory and somatosensory treatment

Chapter 5 - From Calm to Explosive: the HSC Anger

Does your highly sensitive child get angry frequently? Do they go straight from calm to explosive with no warning? Are they quick to get upset about things that others seem to brush off easily? Highly sensitive children (HSCs) tend to feel things more deeply and sometimes those feelings include intense anger. This chapter focuses on anger and the highly sensitive child. I will be explaining what causes angry behavior in a child and offering parenting strategies to help address anger with highly sensitive children.

What's causes angry behavior?

Anger is the behavior that stems from unresolved feelings. It indicates that something is wrong and is the result of another deeper emotion your child is feeling. In order to discover what is causing the angry behavior in your child, you need to dig deeper. Try visualizing your child's emotions as an iceberg. Anger is the secondary emotion they are expressing and that you are seeing, but there is something happening underneath the surface that is causing this anger to be expressed. You need to take a step back and ask yourself what is really going on here? What emotion or discomfort are they experiencing that is leading to this angry behavior. Are they overwhelmed? Embarrassed? Frustrated? Nervous? Disrespected?

Anxiety can easily turn to anger. When a child feels socially uncomfortable or has fears or worries that they can't figure out how to express, they can get pushed down. Eventually those feelings build up and spill out as anger. I created the graphic below to illustrate some hidden emotions that may result in angry behavior.

Look for Patterns

If you are having trouble pinpointing an underlying reason for anger, start recording when your child is having a lot of anger. Are you seeing it consistently before the start of a school day? Does it occur when he or she is frustrated and can't figure something out? Is it frequently happening when they are with a sibling? Really observe your child and record everything for at least a week. There could be quite a few things contributing to a highly sensitive child's anger and outbursts. Recording when these emotions occur can help you discover patterns that will be helpful for moving forward. If you have a better understanding of when most of the anger occurs, you can begin to get a clearer idea of why your child is getting irritable.

Are they getting angry right before leaving for school?

They may be nervous or anxious about something happening at school that day or the whole school day in general. Are they struggling with friendships at school? Is a peer bullying them? Are they struggling in a certain subject? Is the classroom environment too sensory stimulating?

**Do they seem to have angry outbursts out of nowhere
when playing with a sibling?**

Maybe they are feeling frustrated and need help working
through their feelings when it comes to their siblings. Is the
sibling very loud? Are they more chaotic when it comes to play?
Are there feelings of jealousy?

**Are they having outbursts when they don't win a game
or they are unable to master a skill?**

This could be jealousy, frustration and/or embarrassment
masking itself as anger. A lot of this could have to do with age
and maturity level as well.

Strategies to Break the Cycle of Anger with Highly
Sensitive Children

It can be hard for children to learn how to calm themselves
down and gain control of their feelings when anger takes over.
Heck, it's hard for adults to do this too! As anger escalates it gets
more difficult for children and parents to stay calm and think
clearly, so how can you break the cycle?

Start with yourself

If you have ever been taken off guard by your child's angry
outburst, you know how quickly it can trigger you to feel angry
as well. It is easy to take their behavior personally, especially if

you are also a highly sensitive person. Staying calm when you are on the receiving end of your child's anger is a challenging but essential skill to learn as a parent. It make take some trial and error to figure out what works best to keep you calm, but once you figure it out it will be immensely helpful. Matching your child's angry behavior only escalates the situation and often results in guilt on your part.

Avoid impulsive punishment

When a child is angry, it can easily lead to negative verbal or physical behavior. Often this leads parents to immediately resort to punishment. Punishing your child can seem like it will work and it can definitely feel like the right thing to do in the heat of the moment, but it is not an effective long-term strategy. It only teaches them that they are not allowed to feel what they are feeling. It took me a long time to realize that punishing angry behavior was not getting myself or my sensitive kids anywhere. Honestly it made things much worse! They would get angrier for being punished and I would get angrier at their behavior. Then we would end up in a battle that neither of us could win and we would both end up saying things we regretted. Eventually we'd calm down, say we were sorry and it would start all over another day. It was a vicious cycle that didn't solve anything. This doesn't mean that you don't explain right from wrong. You need to be clear that it is never okay to physically or verbally hurt someone else; however, an angry child is not thinking clearly. Their emotions have taken over and impulsive behavior can quickly occur. HSCs often needs assistance regulating those angry feelings. They know that anger can be hurtful, but it is a powerful emotion that is hard to control without help. Angry children need tools to help them cope.

Give them time to cool down

Nothing is going to be accomplished when your child is consumed with anger. Allow your child to feel angry (as long as they are not verbally or physically hurting anyone) and give them time and space to cool down before attempting to talk to them. Let them know that you are there for them when they are ready.

Validate their emotions with empathy

Sensitive children need to feel understood. When they are feeling mad and frustrated they are not going to be in the correct mindset to have a conversation. Instead of jumping in with judgement or shaming, just be there for them. Listen to them and allow them to calm down. What they are feeling is real to them and they need to feel understood. Want some effective phrases you can say when your child is angry? Get the free cheat sheet below!

Give feelings a name

Once your child has calmed down, be sure to label their feelings by saying something like, "I can see that you are feeling very angry," or "It looks like _________ really made you upset/frustrated. This will give them the words to put to their emotions. The more you help them with this, the more they will be able to identify their feelings in the future and communicate them in a more effective manner. For younger children, a feelings wheel or cards showing different emotions can be very useful tools to help them describe their feelings. As a child grows, identifying their feelings through writing and drawing can be an incredibly effective method as well. You could create these types of resources on your own or you can use my Feelings and Emotions Printable Pack which gives you access to all of these tools in one convenient place.

Help your child identify their triggers

If your child is old enough, have a talk with them about what they feel led to their outburst. If you have been writing down their angry outbursts in a log, as discussed in the beginning of the post, talk about any patterns you see. Are they getting angry when they lose a game, when they are not being listened to, when they are hungry or overtired, when they are rushed, right before school or when arriving home from school? Have a discussion with your child and really listen to their responses. It will give you so much insight moving forward.

Come up with a plan

Once you and your child have a better understanding of why and when anger is occurring, create a plan together to manage it. What can they do next time they start to feel anger building up? How can they ask for help? What coping mechanism can they use to manage their anger? Figure out what calming strategies work best for your child and put a plan in place to help them feel more in control of their anger.

Connect and Build a positive self-image

Маке time for one-on-one meaningful connection with your child each day. Children need to feel loved and valued. Be sure to communicate and let them feel your unconditional love. This can be a simple, but really effective tool in limiting anger going forward.

Helping your child кnow how to handle their anger and frustration is one of those difficult but essential lessons we need to teach our children. It's окаy for children to feel angry, but it is important for them to learn how to express and manage those emotions in a healthy way. At this point, you should now have a better understanding of what causes anger in a child and have some parenting strategies to address anger in your highly sensitive child. When you start seeing anger for what is truly is, you can begin to help your child manage it more effectively.

Chapter 6 - Highly Sensitive and Autism: Similarities and Differences

High sensitivity is often compared to autism. This can be surprising: the signs of the two traits are very different. But both have been treated very similarly by the general public. Just as autism is now increasingly seen as a healthy trait, being an HSP is not a disorder, and it's a trait found in up to 20 percent of the population. Both also come with a ton of advantages. In the case of high sensitivity, that includes empathy, compassion, creativity, and the intuitive ability to see connections that others miss.

The similarities go deeper than that, however. For example, both autism and being an HSP can involve extreme sensitivity to your environment. Any highly sensitive person understands what it's like to have the world "turned up too loud," and many autistic individuals have that same experience—especially about seemingly "small" stimuli, like the rub of clothing texture or an intrusive noise.

Likewise, both HSPs and individuals with autism tend to get overwhelmed by environmental stimuli. Autistic children, for example, may panic, have a tantrum, or "shut down" in response to overwhelming stimuli, and many HSP children will do the same thing when they get overstimulated, especially if their parents haven't taught them good strategies to avoid overwhelm.

But, despite those similarities, autism and high sensitivity are two different things. Not only that, but a recent study shows they are profoundly different—and that high sensitivity is also unrelated to various disorders, such as schizophrenia and PTSD. It suggests that being a highly sensitive person is a normal, healthy trait.

What Makes Autism Different From High Sensitivity?

The study, led by Dr. Bianca Acevedo of the Neuroscience Research Institute of the University of California, is an exhaustive analysis of 27 papers comparing high sensitivity, autism, and other conditions. (You can read the full study here.) It refers to high sensitivity by its formal name: Sensory Processing Sensitivity or SPS.

The study also refers to autism as Autism Spectrum Disorder, and uses some language that I think many autistic people would disagree with. I'll just say up front that many people argue that autism is highly advantageous and should not be classified as a disorder at all; a fair amount of research agrees, including evidence that autism may correlate with high intelligence. Acevedo and her team found three major differences between SPS and autism:

1. Autism comes with "social deficits"; high sensitivity does not.

Acevedo's research noted that autism comes hand-in-hand with so-called "social deficits," such as difficulty making eye contact, recognizing faces, responding to others' emotional cues, and reciprocating another person's intentions (think of smiling back at someone who smiles at you). For autistic individuals, the social deficits are obvious as early as two or three months of age, and they're directly tied to how an autistic person's brain works—they tend to show less response in brain areas associated with empathy, social cues, and self-reflection. (One reason for this may be that autistic individuals have very different body language than neurotypical individuals, and they don't get to "mirror" people with their own body language nearly as much as neurotypical children. In other words, this so-called "deficit" may be much more of a lack of opportunity than an innate part of autism.)

For SPS or high sensitivity, exactly the opposite is true. Highly sensitive people don't show social deficits; in fact, they tend to be highly responsive to social cues, facial expressions, and the intentions of others. Likewise, the same areas of the brain that are less responsive among autistic individuals tend to be very active for HSPs, who present high levels of empathy, social awareness, and self-reflection.

2. For highly sensitive people, social situations are (extra) rewarding.

Human beings, in general, are wired to find social interactions rewarding. This encourages us to form strong bonds, help each other out, and cooperate with one another; it's always been a key to our survival. Highly sensitive people are no exception, and may even respond more strongly to social interactions than others do—feeling anywhere from calmed to downright jubilant about a positive interaction. People with autism, however, experience social interactions differently. For them, Acevedo's study points out, there simply isn't as much of a sense of reward, calmness, or emotion involved in socializing. An exchange with another person may get their attention, but not necessarily feel meaningful. The study says this further affects their ability to respond appropriately to others.

Interpretation matters a lot here. To be clear, autistic individuals can and do form deep, meaningful relationships like anyone else. The difference is in how rewarding they find social interaction, in its own right. Whereas it's extra-rewarding for HSPs, it is less inherently rewarding for autistic people.

3. Their brains handle stimuli in dramatically different ways.

Given that both HSPs and autistic individuals can be extremely sensitive to stimuli, it's no surprise that they do share some areas of high brain activity in common—specifically areas related to attention and reacting (physically or mentally) to stimuli. But that's about where the similarities in brain activity end.

The highly sensitive brain, for example, shows higher-than-typical levels of activity in areas related to calmness, hormonal balance, self-control, and even self-reflective thinking (the ability to process one's own actions and feelings and come to deeper conclusions about them). These go hand-in-hand with a greater level of empathy and depth of processing that define high sensitivity. All of these are either positive, useful traits or can be good or bad depending on the situation.

And all of them contrast starkly with the autistic brain, which Acevedo found to be less active when it comes to the brain regions related to calmness, emotion, and sociability.

High Sensitivity Is Incorrectly Compared to a Variety of Disorders

High sensitivity is also sometimes compared — wrongly — to various mental health disorders. The big ones are schizophrenia and post-traumatic stress disorder (PTSD). These two conditions have little in common on the surface (with each other or with being an HSP), but all of them can involve increased sensitivity to sensory stimuli.

Acevedo and her colleagues delved into these disorders, too — and it turns out that none of them are connected to high sensitivity.

For starters, schizophrenia has even less in common with high sensitivity than autism does. Like autism, it comes without any of the increased empathy or self-reflection that HSPs exhibit, and unlike autism, it has almost nothing in common with high sensitivity when it comes to brain activity. (Also, although not mentioned in the study, unmanaged schizophrenia almost inevitably causes major problems in a person's life and relationships; high sensitivity does not).

PTSD is a bit trickier, because highly sensitive people may be at higher risk of developing PTSD if they go through some kind of trauma. But PTSD patients show none of the enhanced activity in areas related to calmness, self-control, or social awareness that highly sensitive people show, and they suffer a variety of symptoms that HSPs without trauma do not. Disruptions in a PTSD sufferer's brain, for example, tend to affect their memory and their ability to integrate new information. These abilities—and the capacity to process information in general—are actually strong points for a highly sensitive person.

It makes sense why researchers would look for a connection between these various traits and disorders. After all, if they all involve some kind of increased sensitivity, it's worth checking whether they work the same way in the brain — especially if that could help people.

What's fascinating about this research, however, isn't just that it showed that these things have almost nothing in common with being a highly sensitive person. Frankly, if you know any HSPs, you probably could have seen that one coming.

No, what's interesting is what else this study suggests. It doesn't just say that being an HSP is "healthy" or "normal." Rather, at every step, it practically trips over the fact that high sensitivity is strongly beneficial. Being an HSP comes with heightened brain activity in useful brain regions; a strong association with desirable personality traits; and even a tendency toward positive, useful, prosocial behavior.

I think the study's own conclusion says it best: "We suggest that adaptive SPS strategies involving empathy, awareness, calmness and physiological and cognitive self-control may serve a species by facilitating deep integration and memory for environmental and social information, which may ultimately foster survival, well-being, and cooperation."

In other words, your child high sensitivity might be an evolutionary advantage — one that helps our entire species.

PART II
Best Parenting Strategies in Practice

Chapter 7 - HS in Boys and Girls

Is HS more common in females? Nope. Does this surprise you? The trait is equally divided between males and females, but we have to consider that unfortunately, in today's society, expressing emotion and sensitivity is a much more acceptable behavior for a girl than a boy, thus you see it more frequently.

Our culture, particularly here in America, is hostile to sensitivity. We live in a society that disdains sensitivity so that sensitive boys are bullied and misunderstood. The sensitive boy who reacts deeply to stimuli and exhibits emotional sensitivity is perfectly normal. However, there's something wrong with a society that shames males who do not act in a tough, aggressive, and emotionally repressed manner – especially when such a significant portion of the population simply isn't cut out for or comfortable with these behaviors. When sensitive boys do not conform to the stereotypical 'boy code' and instead express compassion, gentleness, and vulnerability, they are frequently ostracized and humiliated. The world and all of its people and species would be better off if every culture valued gentle thoughtfulness in its men. It's time for society to recognize that 20% of our boys are highly sensitive, or have a "finely tuned nervous system", and to give them the support, skills, and love that they need to grow into strong, happy, confident men.

This is where supportive and effective parenting is crucial. Parents, especially fathers, need to take the time to understand and embrace their sensitive boys. Taking the right approaches will help sensitive boys thrive!

A highly sensitive boy has trouble screening out stimuli and can be easily overwhelmed by noise, crowds, and time pressure. The HSB (highly sensitive boy) tends to be very sensitive to pain and violent movies. He is also made extremely uncomfortable by bright lights, strong smells, and changes in his life. The highly sensitive boy's nervous system is 'wired' in such a way that he is more acutely aware of, and attuned to, himself, other people, and his environment   The highly sensitive boy generally reacts more deeply and exhibits more emotional sensitivity However, the degree of emotional and psychological reactions varies in each boy. For example, one HSB may not be bothered by noise or crowds but is made uncomfortable by strong smells and scratchy fabrics. Although the trait has a high correlation with introversion, approximately 30% of HSBs are extroverts. Most boys are taught from an early age to act tough and repress their emotions. In particular, sensitive boys learn to deny their real selves in order to be accepted and approved of by their peers. This denial can create fear, anxiety, and low self-esteem.

If boys express emotions such as fear, anxiety, or sadness, they are commonly seen as feminine. The effect on males of having to conform to wearing a tough-guy mask creates suffering on both a personal and societal level and is particularly devastating for the sensitive boy, who has to try harder than the average boy to repress his emotions.

Positive Traits of the Sensitive Male:

- Compassion
- Gentleness

- The ability to act as a peacemaker
- Concern about the humane treatment of animals
- A sense of responsibility
- Conscientiousness
- Creativity
- The tendency to feel love deeply
- A great intuitive ability
- An awareness of his unity with all beings
- The ability to have and appreciate deep spiritual experiences

Your son is in good company, sharing these traits with such famous highly sensitive males as Abraham Lincoln, Carl Jung, and Wolfgang Amadeus Mozart.

So what can you do as a parent?

Recognizing these positive tendencies and abilities in your boy will give you the opportunity to support and even celebrate him. Children of such supportive parents develop high self esteem and will uphold the highest values in society. A positive and secure bond of attachment between mother and son is important in any family but is essential for the sensitive boy. There is a societal myth that boys don't need as much love and protection as girls. Even with infant and toddler boys, there is a strong belief out there that we should encourage them to be tough and avoid "coddling" them. Hence, boys are frequently forced to separate from their mothers too early as society encourages them to become physically and emotionally independent of mom at an early age. Without the model of a strong connection with the first important woman in their lives, some men who experienced a lack of early childhood nurturance don't quite know how to bond with women later on. Mom has a pivotal role in helping her son feel that he is a worthwhile human being, in spite of messages that he may receive from his peers, teachers, and the media that there is something wrong with him. At times, this may feel like an added responsibility, but it's also a wonderful opportunity for moms to share a special closeness with their sons and actively participate in helping them flourish. Your sensitive son will easily notice subtleties in your interactions with him, so even if you are supportive of your son, it's important that he really knows hat you deeply understand and appreciate his sensitivity.

However, we must also be careful not to become too overly protective. A mom should encourage her son to engage in outside activities with other children while making sure that he feels safe in those ventures. When a mom encourages her sensitive boy, even if he has challenges outside the home, his mother's love and support will live in his heart forever, and he will be able to grow into a more confident man.

It's important that everyone involved in his care is educated on your son's sensitivity, including grandparents, daycare workers, teachers, nannies, family members, and babysitters. Explain the trait of sensitivity to them and ask that they be respectful of him. If you suspect that anyone who cares for him is being disrespectful or harsh with him, take action on behalf of your son.

Your sensitive son can learn a lesson better when he is calm and receptive, so when you are disciplining your son, it's vital to talk to him in a gentle manner. If mom (or dad) screams at her sensitive boy when he misbehaves, he will become more frightened and upset by her anger than a non-HSC. Sensitive boys generally tend to feel guilty when they make mistakes, so there is no need for harsh discipline. It also helps when disciplining the sensitive boy to encourage him to express how he's feeling and to ask him to express what he wants. For instance, you could ask him to repeat, "I'm feeling frustrated since I want to play with my car instead of putting my coat on." This technique helps your son move from being overwhelmed by emotions to knowing how to manage them.

Specific guidelines to help you on your way

Fortunately, with the right support, these boys can not only overcome their challenges but thrive as kids and adults. Here are a few ways you can support your sensitive boy.

A good environment is key

Home must be a sensitive child's safe haven. They quickly pick up on tensions between parents and can be deeply hurt by siblings who tease.

The best thing you can do for your sensitive son is to create a home atmosphere that is warm, soothing, and accepting. Do not allow siblings to tease or name-call. Work to create a home culture where family builds each other up and supports one another.

Here are a number of ways to do this:

- Build positive relationships through dinners at the table, cooperative games, traditions, light-hearted conversations, and quality family time.
- Do not compare siblings but celebrate the uniqueness of each child.
- Make clear rules about treating one another with respect and kindness. When a child breaks this rule, the "consequence" is that he must make amends and repair the relationship. This comes after a heart-to-heart discussion about how he made his sibling feel and why it is important to make amends.
- Keep conflict to a minimum. Though any child may be alarmed and frightened by [hearing parents quarrel], highly sensitive children are likely to be affected even more by parental conflict."

Maintain a secure attachment

A positive bond between mother and son is important for all boys, but it is especially essential for the sensitive boy. There is a societal fear of raising "mama's boys" and of coddling, which lead us to prematurely separate from our boys. Mom needs to remain emotionally connected to her sensitive son.

He will receive many messages outside the home from his peers, teachers, media and coaches that there is something wrong with him, that he needs to toughen up and "be a man," but you are there with the consistent message of you are wonderful how you are. You are a worthy and loved human being.

Here are some tips for remaining close:

- Play. This is the easiest way to connect heart-to-heart
  with any child. Play looks different in the tween and teen
  years. Instead of playing trains or blocks, it might look
  like video gaming, canoeing, bike riding or learning about
  his comic book collection. They key is to get into his
  world.
- From hugs and snuggles to fist bumps and hair ruffles,
  stay connected through physical affection.
- Laugh together. Laughter is the closest distance between
  two people." Shared laughter strengthens relationships,
  so find something funny!
- Be his light reflector. Celebrate your son's many
  wonderful traits. See the good in him and tell him what
  you see, because there are enough people out there who
  will tell them what they see wrong with him. It is our job,
  as mothers, to tell them what we see that's right and good
  and true.
- Avoid harsh discipline and criticizing words which are
  very wounding to sensitive kids. Rather than shaming or
  physical discipline, opt for discipline that connects.
  However, also avoid being permissive for fear of
  wounding your child. Correct him, just do so gently.

Teach him how to handle his strong, deep emotions.

Sensitive boys feel all emotions more deeply than the 80% non-
highly-sensitive population, so it's crucial to teach your son
about his feelings and how to cope with them.

It's really important to not make him feel like he's weird or
wrong for having such deep emotions. I think that it's also
important to validate but not exaggerate his experience. For
example, validating is, "I know it hurts when you stub your toe.

I'll get you some ice" while exaggerating is "Oh my poor baby! That must hurt so much. Let me see! That looкs really, really painful. I see why you're crying! It really hurts, doesn't it!"

I'm speaking from experience; the latter only maкes the situation worse!

Here are some tips for helping your child handle his emotions:

- Use time-in rather than time out. The time-in toolкit will help you create a calming space to regulate emotions and teach about them.
- Teach them how to taкe big deep breaths, hug their Calm Down Companion, watch a swirling glitter jar, and journal or draw their feelings to help them through tough moments.
- Use games and activities to teach about feelings.

Teach him to set boundaries

Sensitive children often are people-pleasers and perfectionists. They go above and beyond to maкe everyone around them happy and comfortable, and sometimes they stretch themselves too thin or put the needs of others ahead of their own too much. Teach them that setting boundaries doesn't maкe them selfish and that's окay (even beautiful) to be flawed and imperfect.

Here are a few ideas:

- Give them scripts to say to their peers when they need out of a situation.

- Give them a voice in your home so they can find their voice outside of it.
- Teach them to trust their intuition and honor their instincts.
- Role-play situations where they might need to enforce a boundary.
- Look for children's books on boundaries, like No Means No.

A word of caution

It can be difficult to not overprotect these boys. It's a fine line I still learn to walk every day—figuring out just how much he can handle and the best way to support him without stifling his growth. There isn't a perfect answer, and I know sometimes I get it wrong. Being overprotective sends the wrong message though—it says I don't trust you to be able to deal with this.

I suppose the best message we can try to give our sensitive boys is I believe in you and your ability to fly, and I'm here to catch you should you fall.

Chapter 8 - Anxiety under control

Anxiety is a surprisingly common problem in children. If your child has sensory processing issues or sensory hypersensitivity, you may have already witnessed how these can bring about or intensify anxiety. These sensory issues aren't always limited to one type of sensory input. Hypersensitivity can be found in any sensory system, and affect a person in one, two, or several systems at once. The intensity of experience common to sensory hypersensitivity, sensory processing issues, or other sensory issues can be a challenge for anyone, but for a child it can be overwhelming.

For instance, to children with tactile hypersensitivity, a sock seam might feel like the scratchy side of Velcro on tender skin. A voice that seems perfectly normal to most people might be painfully loud. Children who experience sensory input this intensely may naturally avoid or try to delay situations where they will be overstimulated by the offending sensations.

Anticipating future situations like these naturally leads anxiety-prone children to worry. A child may worry so much that anxiety becomes a day-to-day response. As parents, we are in a very good position to help our children avoid these pitfalls, and to develop good-feeling, healthy habits and attitudes. There are many positive and healthy ways to manage anxiety that stems from sensory issues. Three examples of anxiety neutralizers are understanding, fun, and mindfulness.

Understanding

Understanding is key—both understanding oneself, and feeling understood by others. Understanding the relationship between one's own hypersensitivity and anxiety can be empowering for children. Feeling understood by others, especially by parents, makes a big difference. Both of these will ease fears, and as parent, you are in the perfect position to help.

Feeling Understood

Children need to know that their parents understand where they are coming from, and that they are not being judged. Parents can ask questions, acknowledge their children's feelings, and help them develop an action plan.

For example, if your child has a fear of leaving the house before school, listen carefully to your child and seek out the underlying problem. Convey that you understand. Help your child express herself using words, so that instead of reacting to her anxieties with a tantrum, she can explain the discomfort. Feeling understood helps your child feel nurtured and supported, and helps promote positive coping skills.

Self-Understanding

Likewise, your child needs to understand himself. Educate your child about his brain function. Explain that a special part of his brain works to keep him safe. When this part of the brain gets a message from a sensory organ (such as the skin, eyes, nose, tongue, or ears), it responds accordingly. For instance, when nerves on his hand send a message to his brain that the stove feels hot, his brain responds quickly by moving his hand away from the heat. Likewise, if his brain receives a message that something seems wrong or unknown (like intense smells, loud sounds, etc.), his brain does its best to understand (interpret) the sensory information and respond in ways that might keep his body safe. In people with hypersensitivities, the signals from the sensory organs send some messages to the brain that are intensified, amplified, or confusing. This is why the brain might send a message saying "Be anxious!" to the body so that it will be ready to run, hide, or maybe even fight.

Just knowing the cause of anxiety won't make it go away, but it's a beginning. Your child may need the support of a licensed, qualified therapist to develop positive and healthy coping skills, but learning to pay attention to their own feelings when anxious can be very helpful right from the start.

Fun

The sensations linked to having fun can be powerful against worries and sensory intensities. Fun is not a direct antidote to be applied during an emotional crisis or time of heightened anxiety, but rather a component to build upon and reinforce. Habitual anxiety can distract a child's natural inclination toward play, humor, and wonder. Facilitate your sensitive and anxious child's sense of adventure. Point out when you notice joy and positive feelings. Laugh together (but never laugh at your child). Identify and help your child find humor, and use a sense of humor as a positive coping skill.

Serenity, feeling calm and at peace, is the opposite of anxiety. One way serenity can be found is by breathing naturally and being fully present in the moment. This type of focus on the here-and-now is called mindfulness. Presence of mind comes with practice. For some, mindfulness is second nature. For the rest of us it's a state we can learn to live in. There are specific skills and habits that can be adopted to build a more mindful way of living. Mindfulness techniques have been proven to reduce anxiety, which in turn can reduce the intensity of sensory overstimulation. It is worthwhile to make time to teach your children how to focus on the present moment, and to be more mindful.

Learning about your child's sensitivity or anxiety, communicating your understanding and support, and focusing on positive feelings can go a long way toward promoting excellent mental health. Your attitude as you travel this path is very powerful. Hold firmly the belief that your child can find peace and calmness. This can generate confidence and mastery. Your approach will be reflected in your attitudes and expectations, which can encourage your own efforts and help your child better cope, overcome difficulties, and ultimately thrive.

Chapter 9 - Negative Self-Talk

Does your sensitive child engage in negative self-talk? As a parent it is heartbreaking to hear your child putting themselves down. Everyone engages in self-critical behavior from time to time, but if negative self-talk is occurring frequently with your child, it is important to address it head on. If left alone, it can lead to a vicious cycle of negativity and low self-esteem. So how can you address this? Here are 8 ways to respond to your sensitive child's negative self-talk.

1. Acknowledge feelings and empathize

Acknowledge your child's feelings, not the words. Really listen to them and discuss the situation together. Underneath your sensitive child's negative self-talk, lies some big feelings that need to be addressed. No matter how ridiculous or embarrassing you believe their feelings to be in any given situation, it is very important to empathize and help them work through it.

For example if your child is saying "I'm so dumb" when working on math homework after school, your immediate response might be something along the lines of "No you're not. You just have to focus!"

Instead of fighting against their words, take a step back and figure out the emotion they are likely feeling when they say these words. A better response would be, "I see you are feeling frustrated when you can't figure out the math problem. I have seen you work through math problems before and I know you can figure out this one too. What part are you stuck on? Let's see if we can work on it together." Let your child know that it is

okay to have challenging feelings but that they do not define
them.

2. Figure out the source

Have an open discussion with your child to trysensitive child's
negative self talk and draw out where these negative feelings are
coming from.

Is someone at school giving them a hard time? Do any of their
friends engage in negative self-talk? Are they having a
particularly challenging time at school or in another area of their
life?

Take the time to evaluate your mindset as well. Children take
their cues from their parents, so it is important to take into
account how you react to challenges and speak about yourself
and family members.

3. Ask for specifics

When a child is engaging in negative self-talk they tend to be
consumed by all-or-nothing thinking. They are seeing things as
black and white with no room for gray. Either 'I am good at this'
or 'I am bad at this.' Something is great or horrible, smart or
dumb, success or a failure. They speak in absolutes like, All the
teachers are mean to me, and I'll never be good at ________.

In order to break this pattern, you need to ask for some specifics
to back up their claim. For example, if your child is saying, All
the teachers are mean to me, ask them to provide you with
specific instances of when teachers have been mean to them.
You could say something along the lines of, "I understand that
you are feeling hurt by your teachers. That would be frustrating.
Can you tell me about some times when teachers have been
mean to you."

This helps break down the all-or-nothing thinking. As your child tries to explain when teachers have been mean to them, they may realize that there has only been one or two instances they can think of and it doesn't involve every teacher. You may also discover that what your child is labeling as "mean" is really a teacher's attempt to help your child do something that is challenging for them.

If your child is saying things like, I'll never be good at soccer, math, making friends, etc. be sure to point out times where they have done something well in that specific area and help them change their thought pattern by adding the word "yet." I'm not good at soccer yet, but with practice I can get better.

I may not be able to do this type of math yet, but if I work through it with someone I will learn how to do it. Having an open discussion with your child and getting specific allows them to see that there are more than just two options.

4. Share your struggles

It is important for your child to know that they are not the only ones who face challenges and struggles in life. Let them know what is hard for you and share specific instances when you have failed and how you have overcome specific obstacles. Make a point to acknowledge when you mess up or make a mistake. This helps normalize the struggle and lets them know that they are not alone when it comes to challenges.

5. Offer unconditional love and support

Providing a loving, supportive home environment for your child is key to helping your child work through their challenges. It offers a safe place for them to fail, try out new things and be themselves without judgement.

6. Focus on their strengths

 As a parent, it is easy to spot negative behavior and focus on things our children are doing wrong. Many times we are quick to point out what they are not doing (cleaning their room, forgetting their manners, etc) and forget to praise them for their good behavior.

Don't feed their inner critic. If your sensitive child is engaging in a lot of negative self-talk, make it a priority to point out their good efforts and attitude. Be as specific as you can when praising your child and celebrate their strengths to build their self-esteem. Make a list of their strengths together and hang it up so your child can see it each day.

7. Rewrite the conversation

Help your child edit the negative script that is running through their head. Give them specific positive affirmations to say when they feel negative thinking creeping in.

If your child is saying, Math is so hard. I'm so dumb. I can't do this! Give them a new script. I am trying my best with math. It is okay if I make mistakes. Mistakes are how you learn.

8. Get outside support

If your efforts to help your child are falling flat and negative self-talk is continuing or increasing, it may be in your child's best interest for you to seek help from a mental health professional.

Chapter 10 - Focus on Feelings, Not on Tears

You may notice that your child frequently cries over little disappointments as if they were huge problems. He/She throws a tantrum because he/she can't find the shoes he/she "needs" to wear. You bought the "wrong" kind of cereal bar for him/her school snack. For these little problems, he/she goes from 0 to 60 — fast. As a result, your child doesn't learn to prioritize big and small issues, doesn't learn to manage ordinary disappointment and causes herself undue stress, and faces social problems when she melts down publicly.

Elementary school-age children occasionally get disappointed when something doesn't go their way. Young children can even get their heart set on small things because they loom large in a child's world; they may then feel crushed when things don't work out. But when your child chronically melts down over small letdowns or setbacks — when little deals are all big deals — then it could indicate your child is struggling to develop emotional regulation skills.

Emotional regulation is one of our executive functions: the set of skills that let us effectively execute daily tasks.

Solution: Validate disappointment

Your child's tears over small stuff is related to emotional control. The tears themselves should be thought of as neutral — there's nothing either good or bad about them. Verbally acknowledge your child's sadness or disappointment, but you don't have to do anything. The parent doesn't need to "fix" the problem by "giving in." You want to avoid a pattern where the parent changes their behavior because of crying.

Your child can learn a response other than, or in addition to, crying. Validate her feelings, but remove the attention from crying. Focus instead on redirecting her behavior towards the goal, and ignore additional outbursts. Lavish praise for attempting or accomplishing the goal.

Don't do this: Say, "I'll go to the store and buy the cereal bars you want," and ignore her upset feelings.

Try this instead: Say, "I'm sorry I didn't buy the cereal bars you want and that you're upset. You'll have to find something in the pantry that works until the next time I go shopping."

If your child chooses another snack — even with some crying or whining — that's success. So praise the action. Say, "I can tell that was hard for you, but I'm proud that you found something else you like." Focus on the end goal and give attention to that, not the tears.

Remember: Your child's intense emotional reaction to a little disappointment isn't necessarily tied to sadness; and it's not a measure of her level of disappointment about the situation.

Handle Big Emotions

It is perfectly normal for children to experience some degree of difficulty and frustration as they learn to execute new tasks.

Toddlers can tantrum, school-aged children can yell and argue, and teenagers can ignore instructions. When deciding if executive function weaknesses require intervention, ask yourself: "How frequently is this occurring? How intense is the experience/significant the impact?" If your answer to these questions is "too much," "too often," "I don't know what to do to change this," or "it's only getting worse," you may benefit from a face-to-face conversation to help problem-solve your concern. Effective problem solving will help you clearly identify the problem, goal, steps it will take to achieve your goal, possible barriers, and available supports.

How can you help your child when they are overwhelmed by big emotions?

In the moment of an intense emotional outburst, let them fully express what they are feeling. Allow them to get their emotions out. They are not going to be in the right state of mind to be reasoned with or to comprehend anything until after they have expressed themselves. If you are in a public place, try taking them somewhere quiet to calm down.

Give feelings a name

Once your child is calmed down, be sure to label their feelings by saying something like, "I can see that you are feeling mad, sad, jealous, joy, etc." This will give them the word to put to their emotions. Eventually this will lead to them being able to identify their feelings in the future and communicate them in a more effective manner.

Validate Feelings

No matter how ridiculous or embarrassing you believe their feelings to be in any given situation, it is very important to validate their feelings. Your child needs to feel understood and comfortable with expressing their emotions. Avoid saying hurtful comments like, "Why are you being so sensitive?" or "That is such a silly thing to be upset about." Instead a positive response that validates feelings could be, "I see that you are really upset about (fill in the blank). I understand how it can make you feel (fill in the blank). What could we do next time to make the situation better?

Be mindful of your reactions and stay in control

When you are validating feelings, it is key to stay calm to best help your child. I completely understand that this is so much easier said than done!! Children take their cues from their parents, so it is important to take into account how you handle your emotions. Do you withhold them or lose control emotionally? Are you consciously or subconsciously teaching your child that certain feelings are not acceptable. How does your child's intensity of emotions and outbursts affect you? Highly sensitive children can easily pick up on the emotions of others whether or not they are expressed out loud, so figuring out what can best keep you calm is essential.

As a HSP myself, I struggle with this daily. I have a very hard time when my youngest (my intense HSC) has loud, tear-filled outbursts, especially in public. My body's initial reaction is to start getting frustrated and stressed. It takes a lot of effort to reel in my own emotions and take a step back. I often find that going to the bathroom or my room for a few minutes where my HSC cannot follow me is the best way to gain control over my actions. I take a few deep breaths and gather my thoughts before I face him.

Honestly, some days are better than others when it comes to my response and as parents we have to remember to give ourselves grace for this. I think a lot of parents feel guilty for feeling frustrated or overwhelmed when dealing with their HSC's emotions. Don't be! You're human and parenting is hard! You are not perfect and you shouldn't pretend to be for your children.

When I don't stay completely calm, I make sure to later address my behavior with them if it added to the problem. I also try to label my feelings and explain to them that everyone has trouble staying calm at times. As parents I think we should keep reminding ourselves that when our child is out of control, we need to do our best to stay in control to avoid a worse situation. It won't always happen, but we are a work in progress too!

Don't take it personally

Your child is not intentionally trying to upset or hurt you. They are releasing their emotions the only way they know how and they choose to do it with whom they feel safest with and most loved by... you!

Use tools to communicate feelings

Use visuals to help your child identify their feelings. Depending on their age, they may benefit from feelings cards that illustrate emotions, or drawing or journaling to help them label their feelings and discover patterns.

Putting it all together

By now, it is clear to see that each highly sensitive child is unique. You should have a better understanding of your child's temperament traits and how they are directly related to their intensity of emotions. HSCs feel things more deeply, so they are more likely to have an emotional intense reaction to their experiences. I hope that the strategies provided give you the ability to better recognize the true causes behind your sensitive child's meltdowns and outbursts, as well as the ability to help them with their big emotions.

Chapter 11 - Help Your Child Get a Good Sleep

We love our кids, but if we are being honest, I thinк most of us would admit that we looк forward to their bedtime after parenting all day! Unfortunately, our children don't always feel the same way. If you are frustrated with the struggles that come with getting your highly sensitive кids to sleep, here is why they may be fighting it and how you can end the bedtime battle with three simple strategies.

There are several reasons why a child may struggle with going to sleep. Maybe they are getting to bed too late and are therefore overtired. Perhaps they are not getting enough time to decompress after a busy day of activities and have become overstimulated. Fear is also a factor for a number of children. They are scared of being alone in the darк where their imagination is free to run wild with scary thoughts.

Highly sensitive children (HSCs) often have trouble with sleep because they have a very active mind. It can be hard to calm down their racing thoughts, especially in the evening, when their minds are busy processing everything that has gone on throughout the day. They are very aware of their environment as well, so an unfamiliar sight or sound while lying in their bed can get their imagination going and their adrenaline racing.

The following three strategies can help relax your child and prepare them for the transition to sleep.

1. Routine

Children, especially highly sensitive kids, thrive on routine. There is a calm that comes with order and habits. A predictable bedtime routine is immensely helpful in getting your children to cooperate. It lets them know what to expect each night and helps them feel safe. Young children do not fully understand the concept of time, but they can understand a predictable sequence of events, so creating a specific order of familiar tasks is important. This lets them know what is expected each night and makes your life a lot easier. Let's discuss some of the important elements of the bedtime routine.

- Timing
  First, the bedtime routine should start early enough to ensure that there is no rushing involved. It is important to remember that transitions are difficult for manyhow to fall asleep fast for kids HSCs, so starting early allows your child to ease into the bedtime phase. In our home, our bedtime routine starts 45-60 minutes before bedtime, depending on if they are getting a bath or shower. On school nights, my boys are in bed by 8:00pm, so we start winding down around 7:00pm. An hour may seem like a long time to dedicate to getting your child to sleep, but it pays off in the long run. The great thing about having a long bedtime routine is that your children will come to understand that the act of "Getting ready for bed," doesn't mean that they are immediately going to bed. It is still family time. This will make them much more

willing participants, especially if you build some fun into the bedtime routine that they forward to. So now that you understand why it is important to leave plenty of time for the bedtime routine before your child is actually ready for sleep, you may be thinking, "What time should my child go to bed?" An overtired child is a recipe for bedtime meltdowns, so making sure he is getting the right amount of sleep is essential. Count back the hours for their age from the time they get up for school in the morning to get your average bedtime. Highly sensitive children may need even more sleep than other children. HSCs need plenty of sleep. It is part of their down time. As a parent to a young HSC, it is important to be mindful of how much sleep they are getting and enforce an earlier bedtime if needed.

- Choices
The routine should be tailored to your family's needs and those that give your child choices to feel part of the process. Would they like to get their pjs or brush their teeth first? HSCs like to feel in control and so allowing them to make their own decisions within the limits of a few choices, will lead to more willingness on your child's part.

- Consistency
Consistency is key. Your routine should remain the same, once you figure out what works best for your family. Of course there will be nights that you have a special event or outing that doesn't allow for the same bedtime routine, but overall having an unchanging, predictable order to

bedtime is very important, especially for sensitive children. Consistency keeps bedtime from turning into a power struggle and will help make nights less stressful and more enjoyable for all involved.

2. Relaxing Atmosphere

After the essential tasks of brushing teeth, getting a drink, going to the bathroom and putting on pajamas are done, it is important to create a more relaxing atmosphere that is conducive to sleep. This can start by having your child put away any remaining toys that are on their floor from the day. This will help eliminate distractions. Next, make sure all electronics with screens are off. Dimming the lights or turning off all but one softer light is a good idea as well. Listening to soft music or turning on a peaceful sound machine may also be a good option if this seems to calm your child. These are all cues to your child that it is time to start settling down.

3. Ritual

This may be the most important strategy of all, because it focuses on special activities you and your child can do together right before bed. What you choose is up to you and your child, but activities should be calming and relaxing to get your child's body prepared for sleep. Here are some options that may work for your family. Pick one or two to try out or create a special ritual of your own.

- Reading a few books together

As a former children's librarian, books are a BIG part of our bedtime routine. Reading to children is so important. It builds a child's language, literacy and coping skills, as well as serves as a special bonding time between parent and child. Here is a list of some of my favorite bedtime stories for kids.

- Snuggling and talking about the day together
My highly sensitive children have very active brains and often need to get their worries and concerns out before bed. After reading some stories, my husband or I take a few minutes talking one-on-one with each of them about their day. This can be a very effective way to calm their mind. Just make sure that your child doesn't turn it into a stalling session.

Meditation or Mindfulness Activity

Mindfulness can help calm those busy thoughts in a child's head. A mindfulness instructor recently came to my son's class and taught the children some techniques over the course of a few months. We now incorporate these on nights when he needs more help settling down. Sitting Still Like a Frog: Mindfulness Exercises for Kids (and Their Parents) is a great book that also comes with an audio CD of guided exercises that could be used at bedtime. A few other audio CDs/MP3s that may be helpful (although I have not personally tried them with my children) are Indigo Ocean Dreams: 4 Children's Stories Designed to Decrease Stress, Anger and Anxiety while

Increasing Self-Esteem and Self-Awareness and Indigo Dreams: Kids Relaxation Music Decreasing Stress, Anxiety and Anger, Improve Sleep

Prayers

If your family is religious, incorporating prayers into the bedtime routine can be an important ritual for your children. In our family, we tell God what we are thankful for and pray for others after getting tucked in bed. If you feel more comfortable with more structured devotions, there are several bedtime devotional books available for children. We love the the Berenstain Bears in our home, so I recommend, The Berenstain Bears Bedtime Devotional; however I did stumble upon May the Faith Be With You: Bedtime Prayers, which I may be purchasing soon for my Star Wars/space loving boys!

Singing a Song

A calming bedtime song is another great way to help your child relax. It is also a nice cue that it is now time for sleep.

A Calmer Bedtime Everyone Can Enjoy

Each age will bring new challenges for bedtime and sleep, but with the above foundation you can adjust and move forward. You now have a solid understanding of why your highly sensitive child may be fighting sleep. You also now know how to end the bedtime battle with three simple strategies (Routine, Relaxed Atmosphere and Rituals.) How will you change your current bedtime strategy with your child? What calming rituals will you incorporate to make it a less stressful event? Maybe more importantly, how will you spend your newfound free time in the evening?

Chapter 12 - HS Parent for a HS Child

The baby books I poured over while pregnant all listed similar reasons why a baby might cry: hunger, fatigue, gas. But another big one is overstimulation. A new baby's brain can easily overload when confronted with too much sensory information at once, including noises, new faces, or flashing lights. Even activities that seem enjoyable, like excited older siblings playing with a fancy new electronic toy, can reduce your little one to tears when it all becomes too much.

Now imagine a similar scene, except this time it's you, the parent, who is overstimulated. Maybe you're not quite in tears, but you're certainly feeling a crescendo of tension, edginess, and unease that becomes extremely uncomfortable, if not unbearable. It's all you can do not to shoo the children into separate rooms, chuck that toy (clearly designed by a sadist) out the window, and hide under a blanket. Only you don't, because you're a parent.

Family life is full of awesomeness, but it also has its share of challenges: meltdowns, the headache-inducing din of a busy household, and the stress of shuttling everyone around (on time) to all.the.things. It's normal for parents to feel overwhelmed, sensitive, and even a little fragile from time to time. But what if you feel like this most of the time?

Do you internalize every bit of raw emotion your threenager projects in a tantrum, until your head spins from the chaos and commotion to the point you can't think straight? Maybe you are the one crumbling in the car when you're late for preschool dance class and just can't face the judgmental side-eye. This can be the case for parents who are HSPs: Highly Sensitive Persons.

HSPs have something called Sensory Processing Sensitivity, or SPS. They constitute almost a fifth of the population— 15 to 20 percent. HSPs are highly attuned to themselves, others, and their environments. Although the degree and focus of their sensitivities can vary, HSPs process stimulation and emotion more deeply than the average person. In many aspects of life, this is beneficial: caring for others, reading people and situations, empathy, creativity, and experiencing life intensely. But all this emotion and stimulation can take an acute mental and physical toll, especially if you are surrounded by it daily. (Hello, parents of young children!)

Being an HSP is often confused with being an introvert. 70 per cent are, but that leaves 30 per cent who are extroverts. These individuals find socializing energizing, yet still require solo downtime to process and reset.

Downtime isn't a luxury for HSPs—it's a necessity. It's a way to recalibrate when our systems get overwhelmed. Pre-baby, for me, this meant checking out: leaving a situation, or immersing my attention in something else, like haunting dark corners of libraries, journalling, playing music, or other calming, solitary pursuits. But parents can't check out—it's a 24/7 gig.

Monitoring your physiological stress response helps you identify triggers and be proactive about avoiding—or at least reducing—them. Starting with a comfortable sanctuary makes the added noise of yours son's frequently enthusiastic play more manageable.

But, life isn't always something we can manage. Sometimes your little darling escalates into an ear-splitting tantrum in the middle of the supermarket and you (perhaps already frazzled from menu planning and toddler wrangling) start to feel the burning spotlight of public shame on your cheeks and a rising surge of emotion. What now?

A child's public tantrum is not always such a big reflection on you. Tell yourself things like, "'This is perfectly normal for children to have these kinds of outbursts, because they haven't learned to regulate their emotions yet. These kinds of things are going to happen. I'm not a bad mother if I can't get this dialed down.'"

Parenting is a wild ride, whether you're an introvert or an extrovert, whether you have toddlers or teenagers, whether you're raising five kids or just one. Despite the challenges, you have to be grateful to be an HSP parent. It helps you support your son or daughter and empathize with how overwhelming it must be for him/her.

Chapter 13 - The Challenge of Parenting a Strong-Willed, Sensitive Child: : a motivational story

Miranda says: *"My first strong-willed, sensitive child was my daughter. Shortly after she was born, many described my baby girl as an old soul. As an infant, her eyes were wide with curiosity. With a serious expression on her face, it was as if she was analyzing everything. As an infant, she was a happy baby. However, she got overstimulated easily and was quick to let me know when I needed to take her out of a crowded room. Her first day of preschool was another example of how her personality plays out. She had her backpack ready days before the first day of school. Once she was packed, she was furious she couldn't go to school that instant. When the first day of school came, she lept with joy. When we pulled into the parking lot, she told me to wait in the car and let her walk in on her own. Considering the fact she was three and not thirteen, the answer to that demand was a definite no. I did my best to keep with my two-year-old son on my hip as my little girl burst through the rusty red school doors. In the classroom, her whirlwind of excitement came to a screeching halt as she saw another girl crying. My daughter's desire to leave me in the dust tapered. Her big brown eyes got even darker as the empathy she felt for the girl washed over her.*

"She's sad, Mama."

My daughter didn't know how to reconcile the dissonant emotions. She was excited to leave me while another child was brokenhearted that her mom had left.

Thankfully, this situation acted as an opportunity for both girls to make a friend before class started. (They felt the cloakroom holding hands and were best friends for the rest of the school year)."

Parenting a strong-willed, sensitive child is challenging

If you can relate to examples like these, chances are you find parenting your child to be dynamic and, at times, exhausting. There is no autopilot for parenting these spirited, emotional souls. This is because strong-willed children take nothing at face value. They are forever trying to determine what the boundaries are and will always try to negotiate. Furthermore, these children are acutely aware of changes in their environment, have big hearts, and equally big emotional reactions.

So often, children of this nature pick battles or are devastated over things like:

- being served big carrots you cut for them instead of mini carrots
- you suggesting they wear a pair of pants that "feel funny"
- a change in plans, like having to wait to go to the aquarium because the baby hasn't woken from his nap.

The good news

Strong-willed, sensitive children are naturally equipped with some of the greatest predictors of lifelong success. For one, they are naturally tenacious. In addition to being gritty, these children are more inclined to be leaders and stand up for what's right. Strong-willed children are usually self-motivated and inner-directed, and often grow into leaders as adults. They are more impervious to peer pressure and go after what they want with more gusto. They want to "learn things for themselves rather than accepting what others say, so they test the limits over and over," and this relates to relationships as well. Such discernment involves not only when they cut their hair, eat vegetables, or choose to wear a coat, but also in whom they decide to trust and in whom they choose to follow or who they allow themselves to be influenced by.

5 key strategies that make parenting a strong-willed, sensitive child easier

Frame your child's behaviour. By understanding your strong-willed, sensitive child, you have context for your child's behaviour and are better equipped to coach it.

- **Work with your child's personality by establishing the family rules together**. Call a family meeting and discuss problems as well as goals. Prompt your children to talk about what rules they think are reasonable as well as how they should be reminded when mistakes are made. In this situation, you are still the parent and you are guiding the discussion while collaborating to accomplish peace and cooperation in your household.
- **Frontload as often as possible**. This means to look for every chance to give your child a heads-up before disappointment strikes, plans change, or the going gets tough. This will make it so much easier for her to be resilient when she feels challenged.

- **Make boundaries firm and discipline gentle**.
  Strong-willed children need to know what rules are non-
  negotiable. This minimizes power struggles and also
  facilitates confidence in a child. Research shows that
  sensitive children feel the most vulnerable when
  boundaries aren't clear. Equally, discipline must be calm
  and gentle. Studies on sensitive children show that they
  hold themselves highly accountable for their mistakes. In
  cases of misbehaviour, the best approach is a subtle
  reminder or in more extreme cases a timeout where
  you're with your child.
- **When appropriate and with your child's
  permission, explain your child's temperament to
  others**. Some may mistakenly think your child is
  intentionally being too sensitive or strong-willed. Others
  may not know how to make sense of your child's nature.
  By giving context to who your child is, the adults in your
  child's life will be better equipped to take care of and
  guide him.

A final note on sensitive and strong-willed children
Strong-willed, sensitive children require patience and
consideration. They aren't easy to raise, but their temperament
gives them the innate capacity to become compassionate and
meaningful leaders. The key is to work with their personality
while increasing cooperation. To do so, the adults in their lives
must work with them instead of against them, be clear with their
expectations but gentle with their discipline, and act as their
advocate where appropriate. In doing so, adults are able to guide
the child in a way that celebrates who she is. This then gives the
child to truly become the person she is meant to be."

PART III
Best Tips to Help your Kid Handle this Gift

Chapter 14 - Preschool Time: Getting Ready for School

Preschool is an excellent way to help a child enter the social world outside the home and prepare for the major transition of going to kindergarten. The teachers find HSCs going every day, even if for a short time, so that they have a routine and do not have the transition between whole days at home and at school, loosing some of the advantage of habit and familiarity

After a considering the environment and resources mention your child's sensitivity to the teachers. Some will think your child must be a problem, others will think: "Yeah,yeah, all parents think their kid is special an different. Watch for the teachers who gets it or at least seems willing to listen. Ne sure at this point that almost everything you say about the trait is positive.

Especially if your child Is socially hesitant, ask how the teachers would handle a child who does not join structured group or does not play with other children. You should letting the child take some time, then initiating small steps to help the child join as he feels ready. Perhaps he will be allowed to play first only with the teachers or with one child, then the teachers adds another. Perhaps a groups of two can be formed, then of three, then of four. Observe for the first thirty minutes to two hours, and do this for several days. If you enroll your child you may still want to stay somewhere nearby for few days, so the teachers can find you if she is not adjusting well.

- Talк about separation, so it does not comes as a surprise. But match your emotional tone to your child's, being matter of fact unless she express sadness or dismay.
- Talк about what you will be doing while you are separated, and what you will do when you will bacк together, so your child can experience your continuing existence and relationship
- Let your child таке something from home as comfort, maybe something of your picture of you to кеep in his pocкet or toy.
- Came bacк early the first time, кeep the time short, point out often that you will be bacк.
- Say exactly when you will be bacк in terms or shedule, after your rest time.
- Have a special good-bye routine or ritual, maybe invent a special handshaкe or hug.
- Checк to see if your child is crying more than five minutes after you leave, if the crying continues for more than fifteen minutes or happens through the days for several weeкs it may be too soon for your child to be left. Follow your instincts.
- Once your child is used to your leaving кeep your departures firm, cheerful and short
- Do not rush a separation either. A well-paced departure from home and departure by you at school кeeps the arousal low and leaves enough time for the adjustment
- Remember, returning home is a another transition. Maке coming home enjoyable. Have your child use the toilet before leaving. Talк in the car about what happened at

preschool. Have a snack waiting if your child could be
hungry or thirsty.

- Spend some time at the kindergarten now and then,
  letting your child show what she does there so that both
  of you can talk about it at home.

What Should You Keep in Mind When Selecting a
Preschool for Your HSC?

There are a few factors you'll want to place at the forefront of
your mind during your decision-making process.

Transition Procedures

For highly sensitive children, transitions can be especially
stressful. If your child already attends daycare, you may find
that dropping him or her off is the most hectic part of your
morning. By inquiring into the transition procedure of your
chosen preschool or pre-k program, you'll be better equipped to
decide whether the transitions are fluid and flexible enough to
meet your child's needs or will send him or her into a tailspin
immediately upon arrival.

Many HSC do better with a slow-paced transition to activities-
for example, eating breakfast quietly at a table after they arrive
at preschool rather than immediately being sent into a loud
room with other children playing.

Independent Play

Schools that focus on learning through play and fostering independence can often appeal to the HSC. As opposed to more structured programs where children aren't able to choose what they work on or where they play, these child-centered programs can give your HSC the flexibility to step back when an activity becomes overwhelming rather than force themselves to continue and go through a meltdown.

If you're child doesn't respond immediately to your attempts to help them, don't worry too much. As your child gains independence and forms relationships with his or her peers, the activities that are perceived as overwhelming may become fewer and farther between. Talk to the professionals at Kid's Country for more information.

Chapter 15 - How Can You Help your HSC at School

Deciding where to send your child to school is one of the biggest decisions you will ever make for them. It's also one of the most important! Where your child attends school can make all the difference in their academic and social success, as well as determine their future endeavors.

No wonder this decision is such a source of anxiety for parents! If you are raising a highly sensitive child (HSC) that has sensory or anxiety challenges, the decision can be even more daunting. In this chapter, I will be discussing eight questions you should definitely be asking when choosing a school for your child.

8 Key Questions to Ask when Considering a School

1. What is the average class size?

How many children are there per class? Is there a classroom maximum before it is split into two classes? Highly sensitive children often struggle with noise and crowded places, so the bigger the class size, the more likely they are to feel overwhelmed.

2. What is the student-teacher ratio?

Student-teacher ratios will vary greatly depending on your child's age, grade and school, but it can be a good indicator of a teacher's workload and how much individual attention your child will likely receive. Does the school utilize classroom aides and if so, for what grades? Having an extra adult in the class can make the classroom run much more smoothly. An aide can assist with any emotional or behavioral needs, when a teacher is focusing on lessons.

3. How do you support children with different academic, social or emotional challenges?

Does the school have any formal programs or guidelines in place for helping children work through social or emotional conflicts? Do they offer after-school tutoring or in-school assistance for children struggling in specific academic areas? If your HSC has specific sensory sensitivities that you foresee strongly affecting them in the classroom, be sure to mention these. Are they willing to work with your child to accommodate these challenges when able?

4. What specialists are available at the school?

In going along with question number three, it is important to know what specialists are on hand to help should any issues arise. Is there a school psychologist on-site? A social worker? Speech-pathologist? Occupational therapist?   School districts may group these specialists under a term like 'Child Study Team.'

5. What is the learning environment like?

Does the school take a hands-on, active learning approach? Is the focus more on using technology like Smart boards to convey information? Is there a lot of small group work or do students complete most work on their own? Are there a lot of movement activities? Are there opportunities to have quiet time when needed? Listen to their responses and evaluate them against your child's personality to determine if the learning environment would be a good fit.

6. How many transitions are there throughout the day?

Since HSCs often struggle with transitions, especially unexpected ones, it is important to know how a typical school day is structured. It usually takes an HSC more time to adjust to change than other children, so you will want to find out how frequently transitions occur throughout the day. How much time do they have to transition between activities and locations outside of the classroom? Do most transitions take place within the classroom or are they required to leave the room for specials and other daily activities? How much time do they receive for lunch? Recess? An HSC will typically do best when they receive a good amount of warning before a transition occurs, especially at the beginning of the school year.

7. What is the school's approach to discipline?

How does the school handle challenging behavior? Do they resort to loss of privileges like recess or snack? Detention? What is their policy on bullying? Do they have any anti-bullying education for students and/or staff? Highly sensitive children are typically rule followers. They typically hold in a lot of their emotions at school and often don't want to step out of line; however HSCs can easily be negatively affected by harsh discipline and yelling, even if it is not specifically directed at him or herself.

8. How is information communicated to parents?

How does the school communicate with parents throughout the year? Is email the main method? Text messages? How frequently are parent-teacher meetings held? What is the availability of staff? When calling the school, is a parent sent to a voice mail or directed to office personnel? Are parents able to email their child's teacher directly? Can you request an additional meeting with teachers or staff if needed at any point during the year?

Be your child's biggest advocate

School is a place that your child will be spending the majority of their time each day, so it is important to ensure that your child feels safe and comfortable there. Although it can be difficult or awkward to ask some of the above questions, you owe it to your child to be their advocate in the school setting.

Take notes on what you observe during a school tour and talk to other parents who's children attend the school to get some outside feedback as well. The answers you receive will vary greatly depending on the age of your child and the level of education, but asking these questions will give you some wonderful insight and help you determine the best school for your highly sensitive child.

Leaving behind the carefree days of summer and heading back to the busy school schedule can be a very challenging transition for the sensitive child. Highly sensitive kids (HSCs) need time to adjust to change and a new routine. As a parent, it is important to begin implementing a plan at least a few weeks prior to the first day of school. In the post below, I will be giving you 7 strategies to help your sensitive child with the back to school transition.

Educate teachers and staff

You will need to educate your child's new teacher on the term "high sensitivity," ideally before the school year begins. You want to do your best to inform without overwhelming. Giving them a printable or two on high sensitivity and making them aware of how to best interact with your child is a great way to start the conversation. Make sure that you explain your child's sensitivity in positive way. There are so many wonderful aspects to being highly sensitive and you want to be sure your teacher doesn't view it as a negative "problem."

If you are interested in getting more detailed instruction on how to educate the educators, receiving ready-to-print cheat sheets and an "All About My Child" template that you can edit for teachers, I provide all of this in my course, Making Sense of Sensitivity at School.

Play dates with classmates prior to the start of the school year

If your HSC has trouble socially at school, help him/her develop some friendships through one-on-one playdates/hangouts at your home. Invite children (one per playdate) who are going to be in your child's class for the upcoming school year, so that they can develop/strengthen their friendships with classmates before school starts up. Knowing that your child has a few friends he/she is comfortable with in their class, will help them feel much more confident transitioning back to school.

Get re-aquainted with the school environment

Talk to the principal, director or school psychologist at the school to set up a time to stop by with your child to see his/her new classroom a week or two before school starts. School staff will likely make accommodations for this if they know your child is highly sensitive and has trouble with transitions. A school visit a week or so before the start of school can take away a lot of the unknown and fear that may arise on that first day back.

If at all possible, you also want to set up a time to meet with your child's new teacher for a few minutes prior to the start of school. This is a good opportunity for your child to warm up to their teacher a little bit and for you to give them any quick tips/printables about your child.

Earlier bedtime routine

Start getting back into the school bedtime routine a week or two before school starts. Gradually shifting to an earlier bedtime and wake up time gives their bodies time to adjust to the new schedule before the first day.

Take a test run

Practice the commute to school with your child. If they walk to school, make sure to walk that path with them a few times before school starts. Show them where they will be lining up or going in when they get there. If you drive your child, hop in the car and take a drive to school. Make it clear where pick up will be for this school year. Are they taking a bus this year? While you can't practice riding on the bus, you can familiarize your child with where the bus will pick them up and drop off each way, as well as the route it will likely take.

Prepare the night before

Get as much done as you can the night before, so your HSC can have a calm morning without rushing. Have your child pick out their outfit the night before. If it is new, make sure that they try it on beforehand to ensure that it is comfortable to them. This will hopefully eliminate any clothing meltdowns in the morning. Help them pack their backpack the night before too. You want to make sure that you can be present and calm for your child on the first day as well, so make lunches and snacks after the kids go to bed instead of in the morning.

Go over the "plan" for the day

HSCs like to know what to expect. It helps them feel more in control. Giving your child an outline of what the day will likely hold for them will be very helpful. See if you can get a loose schedule for the first day from the teacher. Lastly, while going over the plan have a discussion with your child and validate any fears that they are having. Make sure that they understand how they are getting to school and who is picking them up, (if applicable) so that they are not worried about this during the day.

A highly sensitive child (HSC) needs the right support to flourish in school. Working out exactly what they need is half the problem. Here are seven tips to help you.

First Days Matter

My son started primary school at the beginning of 2011. It was a rough ride from day one. His first day in school was a drama that will occupy a space in my memory for all time. His father and I had to physically drag him into his classroom. Although the teacher was great with him, for my son she was an unknown entity. He kicked, he screamed and he cried. We left the classroom with the desperate cries of "mama" and "papa" ringing in our ears. I could feel my heart breaking as we walked through the recently deserted hallways. I learnt the hard way that highly sensitive children (HSC) in school need a different approach than other children.

We Learn From Experience

If I'd known then what I know now my eldest son's start in school would have been wildly different. One of his regular teachers was on maternity leave so school filled the void with a stream of replacements. We had no idea which face would greet him at the classroom door. The uncertainty didn't give me a comfortable feeling, let alone my four year old son. My HSC is unsettled by uncertainty, change and new environments. Like most highly sensitive children. If I could go back in time I would go back into that classroom, scoop him up and take him home. It was a sign of things to come. Something no child, nor parent, should have to go through when a child starts school. This nightmare was the morning ritual for his first week. The kicking and screaming in the classroom stopped but the daily tears at the classroom door took weeks to dry up. The reluctance to go to school lasted for months and the tantrums trying to get him back to school after lunch didn't end until the school year did. It is clear, in hindsight, that his teacher and I weren't on the same page from the off. His teacher insisted that the best thing for my son was to throw him in at the deep end and have him come to school full time as soon as possible. My mama instinct said a softly softly approach fitted my four year old HSC better.

Learn From Mistakes

Two and a half years later, my son returned smiling from his familiarisation morning at the new school we had chosen for him. Two and a half years after he first started school I was a much wiser mother tuned in to my son's needs in the classroom – and it helped us find a new school that was more in tune with my son's needs. He is now a 'happy to go to school' (most of the time) eight year old and we haven't looked back.

Here are seven pearls of wisdom I've picked up when it comes to highly sensitive children (HSC) in school.

1. Get It Right From the Start

High sensitivity is not understood in every school, despite up to 20% of children being highly sensitive. If your child is just starting out in school you have the perfect opportunity to get it right from the start. Talk to the school director about high sensitivity and what it means for your family. If you get blank stares or cries of "it's not scientifically proven" (or worse) then move on to the next school on your list.

2. Educate the Educators

A teacher needs to fully understand the sensitivities of your child and the implications for your highly sensitive child in school. Many HSCs need a trusted environment to flourish and will sense if a teacher does not behave genuinely with them. They will be frightened by stern or a teacher that regularly shouts at the class. My eldest told us, once he had changed schools, that he went many times to his former teacher to tell her he felt tired in the classroom. It was his way of explaining that his bucket was full and he needed time out. Her response was that he should go to bed. It didn't help him and he stopped communicating how he felt with her. There was no going back from there. It is imperative that teachers understand that a HSC needs down time and feel quickly overwhelmed in a busy classroom.

What if a teacher really doesn't get your highly sensitive child? If a teacher or school does not embrace your child as a HSC then switch classes or consider other schooling options. If those spending so much time with your child do not take your child's needs seriously then school life could be problematic for your HSC. How can a teacher get the best out of a child they don't even begin to understand?

3. Plan for a Good Start for Your Highly Sensitive Child in School

Assess what your child needs before starting a new school or class. The unknown is often frightening for a HSC so an introduction to the teacher and a preview of the new classroom before they begin at school can make a huge difference. Make a photo book of the school to get your child familiar with the environment before they are in it daily. Ask the teacher to outline how the first day will look. Discuss whether you can stay with your child until they are settled and feeling more confident. If a child starts school with a positive experience it will certainly help in the long run.

4. Be Your Highly Sensitive Child's Biggest Advocate

You will need to stand up for your child time and time again. When your child has been seated in a busy aisle but actually needs a quiet space then speak up. Should your child come home pale and wiped out then talk to the teacher about the school day. If your child spends the evening crying because he is over stimulated from a busy day, communicate with the teacher. As a highly sensitive parent you will have to fight to step outside of your comfort zone to help your highly sensitive children in school.

5. Keep Communicating with Your Highly Sensitive Child's Teacher

Keep all communication channels open with your child's teacher. When a school day goes horribly wrong for your HSC sit with the teacher and work out why. Keep talking. And the same advice applies to your HSC too. Talk to your child daily so they can share their school day with you seen through their eyes. Ask what they enjoyed about their day. Ask what the worst part of their school day was. Establish if anything evoked significant emotion (positive or negative). Help them piece their days together.

6. Trust Your Instinct

As a parent you know your child better than any other person on the planet. If you think your child is under par or has been affected by something at school you will usually be right. Don't rely on a teacher to confirm your instinct. Your child is one of many in a class and it is impossible for a teacher to see and notice everything. Trust your instinct and act on it.

7. Know When to Pull the Plug

Or in other words don't be afraid to admit defeat if your highly sensitive child is not blossoming in his or her current school. There are always other options. Whilst many HSCs don't like change they may well surprise you by positively accepting an alternative, if they feel more at home in a new environment. Luckily I'm speaking from first hand experience. Remember that HSCs feel so much more than other children. These children have a sense for what feels right. They usually know themselves where they feel at home.

It's the end of the school day and you are ready to greet the sweet, happy child you dropped off at school or the bus stop this morning. how to handle after school meltdownsYou are excited when you spot your child. You can't wait to give them a hug and hear all about their day. At first, if you are lucky you may get a nice embrace and a few facts from the day, but before you make it back to your home the whining begins. Then once you arrive home, all bets are off. The wrong question or slightest misstep causes an emotional volcano to erupt and you are left wondering, "What the #$@%!"

 Dealing with after school meltdowns are not easy. Now, if you are wondering why your child is extremely emotional, moody and/or having epic meltdowns that makes teenage drama look tame, then you need to know two things right away.

1. It's not your fault.

2. It's not their fault.

Here I will be discussing what's most likely going on and how to handle after school meltdowns effectively.

School is demanding

frustrated childNo matter the age of the child or actual length of time they spend there, school can be mentally and physically exhausting. It is full of sensory stimulation from the time your child steps foot in the school door. If they ride a bus, you can double the amount of sensory input that is coming in. There are a lot of children, expectations from teachers, rules to follow, noises, new curriculum to process and learn, chaotic lunch rooms, quick lunches and recess to name a few factors that can lead to overwhelm.

It is a lot for any child to handle, but for a more sensitive child it can be extremely difficult. They have to try so incredibly hard to hold it together the entire day at school. By the time the end of the day comes, they have been dealing with loud noises, crowds, smells, transitions, unexpected changes, and all kinds of feelings throughout their day. They can't hold it in any longer, they need to release.

Saving it until they feel safe

Of course they are not going to release all their emotions in front of their peers or teachers who they fear may place judgment on them. No, they are going to do it with whom and where they feel most comfortable. They are saving it for when they are home with you.

Now as much as this stinks, I have really tried hard to embrace the idea that this is actually the ultimate compliment. I know it's hard to think that you are rocking this parenting thing when your 5-year-old is convulsing on the floor after giving him the wrong after school snack or your 10-year-old is slamming her door screaming she wants to be alone, but have faith that you are.

The truth is that they are saving this "lovely" behavior for you, because they feel safe with you and safe in their home. They know that they can show their true feelings and that you and your love will still be there for them when they calm down. Reminding yourself of this can be very effective in keeping you calm during an after school outburst.

Even if you know this and remind yourself of this over and over, when someone is whining, screaming or in full on meltdown mode, your own emotions of frustration and anger are going to eventually get the best of you. So what is a parent to do?

Making it to the other side of after school meltdowns

Now that you know why your child may be having after school meltdowns, let's talk about how you can help them and yourself come out on the other side with your sanity in tact.

Allow them time to get it all out

It is important for your child to be allowed to release their emotions. They need to get out those feelings they've held in all day. Giving him or her time to cry, scream or let it out in a safe way will communicate that you respect their feelings. You should however make sure that they know what is and is not appropriate, discussing this at a time other than after school. Physically hitting, punching, or hurting, as well as verbal threats, name calling, etc. toward anyone in the household should not be tolerated.

Show that you care and understand

If they are in the middle of a meltdown, wait until it is over before trying to communicate with them. Then, get down on their level, offer an embrace and make sure to validate their feelings and comfort them. Spend some distraction-free time together after school doing something that you and your child enjoy. Be present with your child. it will make all the difference.highly sensitive child practice patience

Save questions for later

As tempting as it is to ask your child questions after not seeing them all day, waiting until they have some down time will produce better results. I find that my children are the most willing to talk about their day while we are playing together, at the dinner table and right before bed. What child doesn't want to tell you more about their day if it means delaying their bedtime by a few minutes, right!?!

Feed their belly

Offering your child a snack after school is a great way to help them refuel. They probably haven't eaten anything since lunch and if they are anything like my boys they are probably a little hangry (hungry + angry) ⍰

Give them plenty of down time

You child needs time to unwind after a busy, demanding day at school Give them time to relax. Let them have some quiet time in their room to engage in an activity that they enjoy. If time allows, offer to read them a story or have them read on their own if old enough. Try your best not to schedule anything for directly after school and limit the amount of after school activities they are involved in. It is important for them to recharge after school and on the weekends.

Have an ongoing discussion with your child

Regularly talking with your child or the teacher (if needed) to figure out if they are having any specific struggles at school can give you a lot of insight. Help your child release their worries or fears with the help of a Worry Eater or a journal like My Book of Brave.

Keep track of after school meltdowns

Recording when meltdowns occur can give you insight over time into any patterns that may be occurring. The first month of school might be worse than the second due to settling into a new routine. If you discover that the majority of meltdowns are happening on Tuesdays, maybe something takes place on this day at school that they find difficult.

Putting it into practice

You should now have a better understanding of why after school meltdowns may be occurring with your child and how to handle them effectively. Remember that transitions can be harder for

some kids than others. Even though your child is likely
transitioning from a highly stimulating environment to a calmer
atmosphere after school, going from school to home is a still a
transition that requires adjusting.

Chapter 16 - Friendship: the Most Important Experiences for your HSC

Good friendship is beneficial to all children. It builds their self-confidence, as well as their social and emotional development. HSCs love to play and want to develop friendships, but jumping right into a new situation with unfamiliar people isn't usually their style. They typically need to observe a situation for a bit first and may struggle to keep up with the fast-paced play of their peers. They are more cautious and often enjoy one-on-one play over interacting with a group of children. Sometimes they may also feel overstimulated as a result of a sensory factors such as a high level of noise, a very crowded place, or a particular smell.

Highly sensitive boys (HSBs) who shy away from aggressive play or competitive behavior, may have an added challenge of making friends with other boys. They may enjoy a less hostile and more imaginative play that female friends offer and this is okay. Seeking out children with similar temperaments to your child will be beneficial. You can encourage interactions with other boys and girls, but don't push. They will get there when they are ready.

Child watching others playImagine you were invited to a party by a friend. You decide to go, but when you get there you see a few acquaintances, but really you don't know anyone very well.

Now, what if that same friend who invited you starts pushing you to "Just go talk" to those people as soon as you get there.

"Go talk to them, c'mon. What's wrong? I am sure they are nice. Go ask them if they want to talk!"

How would you respond? If you are an extrovert, this might not bother you much, but if you are more introverted or sensitive to your environment, you'd probably be pretty annoyed with your friend! Maybe you just want a few minutes to observe and warm up to the party. Perhaps you want to hang with your friend for a bit or have them introduce you when you're ready; however all their pushing has put you in a bad mood.

Now change the word talk in those sentences to play and think of how a child who doesn't have the same emotional control and coping skills of an adult would respond. Tantrums, crying, hitting, yelling or all of the above might occur, right? Perhaps they might even shut down and internalize it all. Sound familiar? Now that you know why HSCs can have a harder time making friends, lets discuss how you as a parent can help.

The first steps begin with you

First let's start with managing your own expectations. As a parent, you want your child to thrive in the world and a big part of that is developing and maintaining friendships with peers. It can be extremely frustrating and upsetting to see your sensitive child struggling to make social connections; however it is so important to remember that they can and will over time with loving guidance and patience.

Children look to their caregivers for guidance. You are their role models for how to act and react. Patience, acceptance and empathy toward your HSC are key to helping them. I completely understand that this is often easier said than done! You can't help but feel sad and discouraged when you see your child left out or when other children seem to have no problem joining in and making friends immediately and effortlessly.

Meanwhile your child is miserable, hanging onto you whining about it being too hot, too messy or too (fill-in-the-blank). I have been there. "Why can't you just go play!" has come out of my mouth on more than one occasion, only for me to immediately regret it when my child says "I'm sorry mommy." Cue the guilt. It can be a vicious cycle. Pushing an HSC just won't work. As hard as it may be, don't compare your highly sensitive child to other children. They just need some extra help and patience.

What HSCs need from parents:

- **Acceptance** - A child needs to know they are loved and truly accepted for who they are. They feel things more deeply and need to know that beingLoving dad and son highly sensitive is not a flaw.

- **Validation of feelings** - HSCs don't need lecturing. They often just want someone to listen and validate their feelings. With my younger child, I help him label his feelings when his emotions get too big by saying things like "I see that ______ is making you feel frustrated. You are upset about what happened." Helping HSCs label big feelings can help tremendously.

- **Empathy** - HSCs need to feel understood and know that it is okay to feel the way they do. Listen and communicate that you understand how the noisy birthday is hard for them or that playing with unfamiliar children feels a bit scary.

- **Celebrate small victories** - If an HSC does something on their own terms (not through bribery) it should be celebrated, as long as this makes the child feel good. Did they interact one-on-one with a new child for 30 seconds? This is HUGE! Were they able to sit at the birthday table with other kids? Wow! Make sure to tell them how proud you are. This will help boost confidence and self-esteem.

What they don't need:

- **Pushing and Bribery** - HSCs are not easily rushed or bribed. They need to be internally motivated and given the time to do things on their own terms. This stubbornness may seem like defiance, but their strong resolve will be beneficial as they grow.

- **Threats** - Threatening a child is always a bad idea; however it can really affect an HSC who may internalize their emotions and begin thinking there is something wrong with them.

- **Surprises** - I'm talking sudden changes in routine or the ways things are done. HSCs often have a hard time with change. It is important to prepare your child for any change, no matter how insignificant it may seem to you. When we moved the furniture in our living room to make room for a piano awhile back, I didn't think much about it. We had talked about getting a piano and our boys were excited. It never crossed my mind to discuss the fact that furniture would have to be rearranged until my four year old came home from preschool and started crying and screaming hysterically to put it all back the way it was! Planning a surprise social outing, play date, birthday party, etc for an HSC can backfire. They usually like to know what to expect.

Fostering Friendships

Of course it is important to allow children to follow their own path when it comes to friendships, but sometimes HSCs need a little more support and Group of male elementary school friendsguidance when it comes to interacting with peers. Here are a few ways you can lay the foundation for a successful friendship:

Strengthen their social skills

Help your child understand what good social behavior is and model this for them. Emphasize the importance of sharing, taking turns, and losing gracefully. This preparation will contribute to a more positive interaction with peers.

Provide scripts & role play

As discussed earlier, HSCs often do not like surprises. They benefit from knowing what to expect. If you are going somewhere new, meeting up with distant relatives, or hosting a play date with a new child, try to give them an rough outline of what to expect. This helps them feel more in control of a situation.

Reviewing common questions they may be asked, like What is your name? How old are you? What grade are you in? What is your favorite _________? Practice these questions, so that they feel comfortable answering. In addition, giving them ready made scripts for when they meet new people and role playing with these, will help them feel much more confident going into a new situation.

Define what a real friend is

HSCs need to understand what real friendship means. It can sometimes be hard for them to speak up for themselves, which can lead to them being taken advantage of. Make sure to define a friend as someone who is nice to them and takes turns with their friend when choosing what to play. A friend is someone who lifts them up instead of bringing them down. Disagreements will happen between friends, but for the most part they should feel happy when spending time with friends. Teach sensitive children how to be a friend and remind them that true friends accept each other for who they are and care about each others feelings.

Similar interest

These days it is the norm for children to participate in team sports, but competition can be difficult for the HSC. If they are not interested in competitive team sports, don't push it. They will be much happier and successful making friends when they are doing something they enjoy.

Do they like art? Research art classes for kids in your area. Love music? Get them involved with the school choir, band or music lessons. Into acting? Check out a theater group for kids. Lego clubs are gaining popularity at schools and libraries, as well as cooking programs. Ask your HSC about what they are interested in doing and then check out what your school and community offers.

Partnering and Patience leads to progress

Highly sensitive children have so much to offer, but sometimes they just need some assistance and direction when it comes to making friends. Partnering with your child and being their advocate will produce a happier, stronger and more confident person when it comes to social connections.

Chapter 17 - Sports and Activities for Emotional Health

What is the best sport for a highly sensitive child? That's a common question parents of highly sensitive children (HSC) ask. Why? Because some sports simply don't match highly sensitive characteristics.

Why Seems They Don't Enjoy Some Sports

One trait of being highly sensitive is not enjoying being in the spotlight. Your highly sensitive child may well not perform well under pressure – and that includes group pressure. In fact, a highly sensitive child may well feel overwhelmed playing in a sports team. Having to perform, particularly in front of a crowd, is just too much pressure for many highly sensitive children. The competitive nature of some sports simply doesn't tally with the needs of some highly sensitive children. Some highly sensitive child struggle immensely with contact sports, finding them too physical, rough and aggressive. These are elements that feel uncomfortable for many highly sensitives. Noise may also be a negative element for some children. If you think about how sound bounces around in a swimming pool or a gym hall then it's easy to see why these environments may be uncomfortable for your child. Your child may love swimming, just not in a busy pool. Your child may love football (soccer to those of you in the USA) but not during the winter break when training moves inside to a gym (ask me how I know this....) because it's a more intense experience.

These are some of the reasons why, IN THEORY, a highly sensitive child many not enjoy particular sports or activities.

However, each HSC is different. Each child responds differently to different situations. Some HSCs thrive in a competitive team environment. Others prefer more solitary activities. Some kids, like one of my sons, enjoys both!

Right Sport, Wrong Team

"My son changed his football team because of the team dynamics. The culture within the team and the failure of the trainers to tackle bickering and teasing meant that my son stopped enjoying football altogether. He switched teams and was back on track from the first training session with his new team."

Right Environment

"One of my sons wouldn't even consider joining a football team until we moved to a village and the one local youth team comprised classmates and his brother. The team was then a safe environment for him. So he joined the team and is now playing his third season. He is now with a bigger club, playing with boys he didn't previously know. However, that initial step into football gave him the confidence and the boost to give a new sport a go."

Age

A child's age plays a role in the best sports for them at any particular time. As a child gets older and understands themselves better they are more easily able to identify what it is about a particular sport they don't enjoy. A younger child may meltdown if you try any new activity at all. We tried judo with my son when he was five and it was a complete disaster. He

screamed and cried from the moment he entered the changing
room. The same activity introduced months or years later may
turn out to be the best sport for your highly sensitive child after
all.

Each highly sensitive child is unique

While all HSCs are sensitive to their emotional and physical
environment, they will react differently depending on their
genetic makeup and other variables. Some are introverts. Some
are extroverts. One child may have a lot of sensory sensitivities
or be very strong willed, while others are more emotionally
sensitive. These variations can lead to very different interests
among highly sensitive children.

In an effort to provide a comprehensive list that could appeal to
different types of HSCs, I reached out to my readers and FB
community, plus other highly sensitive communities to see what
sports and activities their HSCs enjoyed the most.   Here is an
extensive list of sports and activities that highly sensitive
children are enjoying in all different parts of the world!

Best Sports for a Highly Sensitive Child

The answer is simple; a sport that your HSC enjoys and is
interested in. The best sport for a highly sensitive child is one he
or she feels safe doing. Taking part in a sport or activity should
never damage your child's self-esteem. As long as your child's
experience is positive then it is the best sport for them. And that,
of course, differs per child. It's important that a child does some
kind of physical activity. It may be a trial and error process to
find the right activity. But that's okay. Take your time. If your

child doesn't enjoy team sports then encourage an individual activity.

Give a HSC time to warm up to a new activity. Let them watch the first lesson or training session. Or the first few. Let them get used to a trainer or teacher and the new environment. Don't give up too early.

Follow your child's interests, not your own. You may love tennis but it doesn't mean your child will. Let your highly sensitive child's interests guide you as to the best sport for them.

Steer your child away from choosing a sport because that is what is expected by peers. This is particularly relevant for sensitive boys and sports that are seen as 'proof of masculinity'. Choosing a sport for this reason will have a negative impact on your child in the long run.

Recommended Sports and Activities from Parents Raising HSCs

Whether you are beginning to try out activities with your child or are just looking for some new inspiration, this list will give you a ton of ideas. There are three lists divided into the categories of group sports, individual sports, and non-sport activities & hobbies. Use this list as a starting point for inspiration and conversation with your own child about pursuing their interests.

Team sports
Team sports

Team sports can be tricky for some highly sensitive children, but other HSCs thrive on them. Here are a few that parents of a highly sensitive child have recommended.

- **Baseball**. My son loves being on the field. He says it's calming and he doesn't think or worry about anything. When he gets a home baseball highly sensitive childrun he feels validated in all his hard work. He's been playing for 7 years (going into our 10th ball season) – Jennifer Marzec
- **T-ball** has worked well for us. It is much less aggressive than other team sports. - Lori
- He loves **soccer**! He loves teamwork and loves when everyone cheers when he makes a goal. – Sarah Hood
- **Swim**, individual and team competition – Jenni
- Team **Gymnastics** - Mary
- **Hockey** and **swimming** work well for our child - Lara

Individual sports and physical activities

It is important for children to be physically active, but that doesn't have to mean group sports or competition. Here are some wonderful physical activities that focus on the individual.

- **Karate**! My son hates the competition and pressure in team sports but enjoys the camaraderie, goals and traditions of martial arts. – Lynne
- **Swim Lessons** – Brittany yoga highly sensitive child activity - Cora
- **Yoga** has been amazing for our daughter! - Liam
- **Dance** – at this stage, it's not competitive and there is a structure which lets her know what to expect. She can interact with others in her class but in a limited way, just the right amount for us. – Katharine

- My daughter's absolute favorite activity is **horse back riding lessons** because she has a true love and passion for horses! She also beams with pride when she is caring for a horse...she can groom the horse, pick up the hooves and clean the bottom of their feet, and help saddle the horse. It has built so much confidence in her and I truly believe she is also so drawn to riding because she only has to depend on herself. Riding has taught her patience and self discipline. It has been the absolute perfect activity for her. She started lessons at age 3 and is now almost 7! I am so happy for her that she has the ability to follow her passion. – Natalie Ernst
- Junior Bowling League - Grace
- **Parkour**! – John
- **Dance**, she lives for it!! It gives her energy, she's talented in it, her perfectionism can be applied – Hanneke Legerstee
- **Ice skating** – Stephanie
- **Dancing and singing** – Melissa
- **Karate**: My son started with using noise canceling headphones, but once he gained confidence and more of a sense of self acceptance he stopped using them. He is becoming a more confident boy with an understanding of the importance of protecting one's heart and mind, and physical self. Also, baseball has been a positive experience for him. – Anna Bassett
- **Karate** – Adessa
- **Non-competetive swimming**
- **Gymnastics** – its not competitive (yet, dont know how she will do or if she will choose to compete). She has extremely supportive coaches, it allows her to wiggle – Robyn Highfill

- **Golf** and **singles tennis** have worked well for our son. – Mike
- **Aerial arts** – she feels confident, strong and independent!
- **Cross fit** for kids has been wonderful for my sensitive child.
- **Taekwondo** has helped my now 10yr old girl, she has done it for a few years now after attempting several other thing unsuccessfully
- **Bike Riding** and **Hiking** – Megan
- **Gymnastics** and **swimming** – My daughter wouldn't leave my side at the playground until she was 3, and at birthday parties she always clung to me. We enrolled her in a casual preschool gymnastics class when she was 3, which she did for a year and a half. It took a really long time and lots of patience to let her do things at her pace, but there was no competitive pressure. In that year and a half her confidence really grew, and now aged 5 I see a huge difference in her confidence. We also enrolled her in swim lessons age 4 1/4. It's a small class of only 3 or 4 kids and she has a wonderful, patient teacher who knows that all kids need to feel trust in her before they will step out of their comfort zone. – Claire
- **Rock climbing**
- **Street Dance** – releases stress, burns excess energy, he gets lost in the music and forgets to worry! He comes alive when he dances!! – Paula
- **Fishing** is something our son really enjoys – Steve
- **Dance** and **Taekwondo** – Naomi
- My HSC is in **swimming**. It has helped his confidence tremendously. It took quite some time for him to be comfortable as he had to go into the pool area and parents aren't allowed in, and it was his first experience

with a "coach" and me sitting behind the scenes. He now walks in so proudly, greetsswimming highly sensitive child all of the staff and has a chat with each of them, and can't wait to start! I think it's a great fit for him as it's non-contact, the group is very small- 3 kids-, and it's not loud and fast paced. – Nikki V

- **Roller Skating**
- **Swimming** or **gymnastics** – individual sports work best for us – Anita
- **Bouldering** – Our daughter is not athletic and is hesitant to step outside her comfort zone. Bouldering can be scary and forces her to overcome fears, to trust herself and also is a great workout that improves her coordination and muscle strength. – Sarah
- **Running** – Depending on your child's age and interests there are a lot of options -non-competetive running club, Girls on the Run, Healthy Kids Running Series, Cross Country – Maureen

Non-sport Activities

If your child is not into sports, there are so many other activities and interest groups that may appeal to your child.

- My daughter loves **theater** because she can be a completely different person who doesn't have to hide behind her sensitivity. – Stacey Ventimiglia piano lessons highly sensitive child
- **Art class** and **ceramics**!
- **Piano** and **singing** – Mel

- **Geo caching club** and **Lego club**
- **Theatre** – Ania
- **Youth group at church** – Sarah
- **Music lessons** – piano
- **Drama** has given my daughter a great boost and gymnastics. – Fiona Scalpello Hammett
- **Scouts** (Cub scouts/Boy Scouts/Girl Scouts) Scouting has been wonderful for my sons. They are learning new skills, challenging themselves and building confidence with each belt loop/badge they receive. – Maureen
- Mine loves **theater**. She is typically pretty introverted but when she's on stage she is totally different. – Bobbi Cantrell
- **Guitar, Pottery**, & **Cub Scouts** – Jill Baker
- **Chess Club** – no touching involved from other kids & quiet – Mandi
- Our son has really taken to choir. – Maya
- **Piano lessons** and **volunteering** at a nearby cat shelter – Alice Reeves
- **Cooking** and **baking classes** have been the perfect fit!

Warm up time

If your child expresses interest in an activity but doesn't take to it right away, do not dismiss it or let them quit right away. It often takes HSCs several days or weeks of observing before they are ready to jump in. I remember my oldest son got so upset about swim lessons the first three times we went, but by the

fourth time, something clicked and he started loving them.
Now, it is impossible to get him out of the water. I am so glad
we didn't give up. Let your child go at their own pace and be
wary of allowing them to quit something too early.

Coaches/Instructors

Unfortunately, a coach or instructor can make or break your
child's interest in a sport/activity. If possible, try to get
information on the coach(es)/instructor before enrolling your
child in something. It is important to know the
coaching/teaching style and figure out if it will work with your
child's needs.

Parenting Pressures

Make sure that you evaluate your expectations for your child.
Parents can easily put too much pressure on their highly
sensitive children to perform. This can especially be a challenge
for fathers with sons. Sometimes parents want their sons to
follow in their athletic footsteps and there is a lot of societal
pressure for boys to be athletic. While participating in sports can
provide wonderful experiences that helps boost self-esteem, they
can also be very challenging for a sensitive child. Keep this in
mind as you help your children pursue their interests. Make a
conscious effort to help your HSC find activities that are
enjoyable to them, even if their interests vary greatly from your
own.

After providing you with a huge list of activities, I would be remiss not mention that you need to be aware of over-scheduling your highly sensitive child. Keep in mind that your highly sensitive child needs more downtime than most children and requires sufficient time to unwind after a busy, demanding day at school.

Take a good look at your child's schedule. How many activities or practices are they attending each week? Make sure that there is a good balance between scheduled activities and free time. Scheduling too many sports or activities will overwhelm your HSC and they may end up hating all sports! All children need time to have free time with unscheduled play and relaxation, but it is crucial for a highly sensitive child's mental and emotional health. Keep this in mind as you explore sports and activities for your highly sensitive child.

Chapter 18 - Positive Affirmations to tell your Highly Sensitive Child

Being a parent to a highly sensitive child (HSC) is not easy. It does not take much to get caught up in your child's struggles and the negative self-talk spiral. Parents' actions and words have a huge impact on their kids, so while it is easy to focus on all the things your HSC is doing wrong, you need to be intentional about reminding them how special and loved they are. Here are 30 positive affirmations to tell your highly sensitive child to build their self-confidence and your bond with them.

- You make me smile.
- I love your creativity.
- It's okay to make mistakes.
- You have a kind heart.
- I believe in you.
- I am proud to be your parent.
- I will always be there for you.
- You don't have to be perfect.
- You are a good problem solver.
- I love you to the moon and back.
- You are a great friend.
- You have an amazing imagination.
- I love spending time with you.
- You are a good worker.
- That's a great question.
- You give the best hugs.
- You can do anything you put your mind to.
- Thank you for trying your best.
- You have great ideas.
- I know you can do it.
- Nothing will ever make me stop loving you.
- You make me laugh.
- I love your silliness.
- I can't wait to hear about ________.
- You are so thoughtful.

- You rock!
- You were very brave when __________.
- You are so special to me.
- I will always believe in you.
- I love you.

Chapter 19 - A True Inspirational Story

I began to realize my own son's sensitivity when he was a toddler. He would easily startle, hate surprises, not want to be in crowds (no big birthday parties, and please do not sing to him!), and was sensitive to noise. He had a slight aversion to scratchy material and tags and was (and is!) a picky eater. I didn't realize then that perhaps the textures of some foods bothered him. He was extremely witty for a 2 year old, and he also noticed subtle changes as said on the questionnaire. If we'd go to a grandparent's house, he could immediately point out what had been moved since he was last there. His sensitivity really became an issue to me when I first started "disciplining" him. I've said before, I started out disciplining him like everyone else I knew disciplined their children with the exception of spanking which always felt wrong to me. I used several methods to "gain control" such as time outs and counting to 3. He wouldn't "just be upset" when I put him in time out. He would literally be heartbroken. Of course, I was told he was just manipulating me so he wouldn't have to go to time out, but I know my child. He wanted to please us. He was doing the best he could at his developmental level. So, when I isolated him for what I perceived to be misbehavior, it affected him on a much deeper level. He felt deep shame and guilt and it would last far past when the time out was over.

Now, that 2 year old is a 6 year old. While I have learned that gentle correction is all that is needed for him, there have still been plenty of challenges. He feels pain more acutely than most, so any small scratch or bruise is an event. He scraped his elbow just a few days ago and you would have thought he'd broken his arm. Just getting a Band-Aid on took a good 20 minutes because he kept saying "I need a minute! I'm not ready!" In a culture that thinks he ought to "rub some dirt on it and get over it," even I find it trying to maintain my patience when he has a fit over a scratch.

He still doesn't like birthday parties. He refuses to learn to ride a bike because he may fall and get hurt. In fact, he is super cautious in all of his play. He is very attuned to the moods of those around him and seems to absorb their feelings and energy. He cries at commercials regarding hungry children and homeless animals. I have to screen his movies. The end of Ice Age was too much. Perhaps the biggest challenge was public school. Kindergarten went okay because his teacher understood his sensitivity and accepted him the way he was. She also used a positive reinforcement system of earning rewards rather than a punitive system of discipline. While there were certainly some tears due to separation, he thrived in Kindergarten. However, in first grade, he became a different child. The punitive discipline system used in that class created a lot of anxiety in him. Even though he, himself, was very careful to "stay in line," he felt for the other children and he was greatly bothered by seeing them "in trouble." The fear of being sent to the principal's office for a paddling   was on his mind constantly, even though I assured him they were not allowed to paddle him. Still, knowing other kids were getting paddled upset him. By the middle of the first semester, he was crying every morning and begging not to go. He was exhibiting some anxious behaviors and, even when he was home for the evening or the weekend, he had a sad and anxious demeanor.

I made the decision over Christmas break to pull him out of public school to homeschool him, and even that provided yet another challenge. I chose a Charlotte Mason-based curriculum, which requires a lot of reading of literary classics. Many of the stories were simply too violent for him. He would asк me not to read words such as "кill" or "die." After one particular history story of a battle long ago, he couldn't go to sleep. Не кept telling me those "bad words" were upsetting him. I had to ditch the entire curriculum and start fresh.

Would I trade his sensitivity? Absolutely not!! While it has presented challenges, he is a special and amazing child. His compassion is humbling. His intuitiveness is amazing. He is witty, humorous, bright, and extraordinarily creative. He inspires me daily, and I tell him often that he is a wonderful asset to this world, and he is.

Conclusion

Let's be honest, sensitivity rarely gets the praise it deserves. The label "sensitive" is often used in a negative way in our society. Have you or your child ever been told that you are "too sensitive?" High Sensitivity is a trait that is commonly misunderstood, because there isn't much discussion about the topic; however it affects 15-20 percent of the population.

As a parent, it is easy to get caught up in the challenges and frustrations that come with parenting a highly sensitive child (HSC); however if you can shift your thinking and take time to focus on all the amazing qualities of your sensitive child you can really begin to appreciate what an asset sensitivity can be.

We need to teach our children that being highly sensitive is not a burden, but rather a blessing. It is not only a positive quality, but a beneficial one as well! Highly sensitive people make the world a better, more interesting place. Remind to your child these 10 reason about why being highly sensitive rocks!

1. You are creative.

Whether your interest is in drawing, painting, singing, writing, dancing, acting, building, sculpting, cooking, crafting, clay, photography, or another chosen art form, you are very talented in channeling your creativity. Your sensitive nature allows you to successfully tap into your inner self and express it through a creative outlet.

2. You are a fabulous friend.

While it can sometimes be challenging for you to find the right friends, once you do, they usually become a friend for life. You are respectful and genuine in your friendships. You care deeply about them and try your best not to hurt their feelings.

3. You can't be fooled.

You are very aware of your surroundings and how others are feeling. The ability to sense when something isn't quite right in your environment and with certain people, comes naturally. You pick up on things that others often miss and can sense when people are not being sincere.

4. You are original.

You think outside of the box. Your talent for thinking up new and creative ideas helps others around you see things in a new way. You have a curious mind that is interested in learning about the world and actively question things to gain understanding.

5. You are compassionate.

You have a strong concern for others and don't hesitate to help when someone is in need.

6. You experience happiness more intensely than others.

While you may feel difficult emotions more intensely, you also feel joy more deeply. When something good or exciting happens, you experience a stronger level of happiness than others. A kind gesture, visiting a place you love or a fun time with friends can totally make your day!

7. You are fair-minded.

You know right from wrong. When something is not right, you stand up for justice.

8. You are passionate.

When you find something you love, whether it be a hobby, sport or other interest, you give it all you've got.

9. You have the best imagination.

With your imagination, the sky is the limit! You are a dreamer who is inventive. You can take every day items and find completely new uses for them with your rich imagination. Creating games, imaginative scenarios and stories comes easier to you than others.

10. You have a deep appreciation for the natural world around you.

Spending time in nature is restoring to you. You enjoy the serenity it offers and are more aware of Earth's gifts, as your senses experience them more deeply.

They are some pretty awesome advantages, right?!? And you know what? You aren't alone. Check out this list of influential people who were/are considered to be highly sensitive.

- **Leaders/Philanthropists**:
  Abraham Lincoln, Martin Luther King, Jr., Malcolm X, Ghandi, Dalai Lama, Mother Theresa, Eleanor Roosevelt, Princess Diana
- **Scientists/Inventors**:
  Albert Einstein, Sir Issac Newton, Thomas Edison, Jane Goodall
- **Writers**:
  Edgar Allen Poe, Emily Dickinson, Robert Frost, Ralph Waldo Emmerson, Virginia Wolf
- **Singer/Songwriters**:
  Alanis Morissette, Elton John, John Lennon, Jack Johnson, Dolly Parton
- **Actors/Actresses**:
  Taye Diggs, Jim Carrey, Steve Martin, Johnny Depp, Anne Hathaway, Mandy Moore, Scarlett Johansson, Nicole Kidman